Leeds Born and Bred

by James Thompson

Dalesman Books 1982

The Dalesman Publishing Company Ltd.,
Clapham, via Lancaster, LA2 8EB

First published 1982

ISBN: 0 85206 707 0

For
Edna and Margaret
Leeds 'loiners' who have shared my life

ACKNOWLEDGEMENTS

I should like to express my gratitude to all who have given so generously of their time in helping me with the preparations for this book.

To all the present-day personalities whom we meet within its pages and who have spontaneously and willingly responded to my call upon them for their kind co-operation I say a heart-felt 'thank you'.

Amongst many libraries and librarians I should like to mention particularly the considerable assistance I have received from Mr Pinder, Mrs Wilman and Miss Curtis of Morecambe Library; Mr Craven and Mr Benjamin of Leeds Central Library and Mrs Heap of its Local History department; and Miss Kathleen Rainford of the reference library of **The Yorkshire Post.**

Many directors and public relation officers of industrialists referred to in the script have been of substantial help, and so too has Laurie Hodgson of the 'Old Cockburnians'; Bernard Shaw, a life-long Hunslet supporter; and my daughter, Mrs Margaret Wellock, who has so willingly typed the mss from my almost indecipherable handwriting.

I apologise for any omissions and trust they are minimal—in other words, I hope there are none. Last but not least, my deep sense of gratitude to my wife who has been most forbearing and patient through all the intricacies of searching and scripting.

Phototypeset, printed and bound by Galava Printing Co. Ltd., Nelson, Lancashire

Contents

Preface

FORTY years ago, coming home on Army leave, however slow and tedious the journey, delayed by blackout and blitz, it seemed more slow, more delayed as we tried to enter Leeds station. There was a perpetual curse on the signalling system. To-day when British Rail boast of their inter-city trains and advanced passenger marvels, it is often as difficult to move without delay into the conglomeration of platforms which have fused the New, the Midland and the Central stations into one oil-soaked mass to form City station. But within minutes of your eventual arrival you step out of the gloom into the hub of the city. By law of opposites you are the more ready to appreciate the sculptures that for generations have welcomed Leeds 'loiners'. You are in City Square where statues serve as a welcome and as reminders of allegiance to the crown, religious principles, scientific achievement, benevolence, and indeed beauty. The Black Prince, an imposing equestrian statue, points an imperious and perhaps remonstrative finger at the City Station. The Black Prince of whom some citizens automatically think as one of themselves, local born, little realising that his Yorkshire connection was limited to his parents, Edward III and Philippa of Hainault, marrying in 1328 at the unbelievable age of 15 and 14 years in York Minster. And we think the enlightened twentieth century delights in early marriage! Behind him, like giant chess pieces on an open air board awaiting their next move (for these are not their original sites) the figures of Walter Hook, clergyman; John Priestley, scientist *and* clergyman; James Watt, inventor; John Harrison, benefactor; and those shapely females portraying beauty, the nude nymphs that, with upstretched arms, have shed light on their surroundings for many a long year.

From here radiate the main thoroughfares to the homes, places of learning, worship, trade, industry, entertainment and sport of Leeds born, or those who after their sojourn in the city found national and international renown. Leeds basks in their reflected glory and is proud of their achievements. It knows, too, that those of past generations and those of the present generation who have shown many ways to fame are but the forerunners of those who similarly will hand on the torch of success.

Since 1974, when the Government in its wisdom (or lack of it, you may think) decided to create new counties, to abolish old ones and to establish 'metropolitan' areas, Leeds has, extended its boundaries. This has enabled me to extend *my* net somewhat and include those who would not have qualified if my mesh had only been of sufficient weave to permit 'loiners' to pass through. (A 'loiner', of course, being by tradition, a man or woman born within the city boundary.) It was obvious, as my research developed that many well-known people had founded their fame on education received in the city, or had made their reputation, or increased it, by work done after coming to reside there. In other words, Leeds had played a not considerble part in their life story. Whom to include and, as one or two of these worthies qualified by success in more than one sphere of activity, under which group to place their story. There could be only one answer—let commonsense decide. If some think I have been lacking in this commodity then I can only plead guilty of trying to do my best and allowing enthusiasm to outweigh discrimination. Even so, I trust that the sincerity of my tribute to these personalities either Leeds born or bred will not be doubted.

I hope that those readers who are under eighteen, facing one of the most important decisions of their lives—what career to choose to make a living—will find inspiration from what these locals have been able to achieve; that those over eighty will enjoy nostalgic musings as they look back over their own successes, and perhaps, the odd failure; and that those between these ages will gain satisfaction in just having some interesting bits of history in their hands. This history is interesting; I trust the compilation can also be so described.

Finally, if your favourite has been omitted console yourself with words of Milton, writing of Shakespeare:

Dear son of memory, great heir of fame,
What need'st thou such weak witness of thy name?

1. Leaders of Industry

Joshua Tetley—Alf Cooke—Victor H. Watson (John Waddington Ltd)—Sir Ernest Woodroofe

CARLYLE had much to say on the subject of industry and industrialists, on work and workers—'Man is a tool-using animal..... without tools he is nothing, with tools he is all.'

It follows that man should be profoundly indebted to Leeds, and to the industrial beehives of Holbeck and Hunslet. There, not only have tools been invented, machines fashioned to make tools, but things made with tools for which man in the Old, New, and Third Worlds is grateful. By the mid-nineteenth century Hunslet *Lane* should have been re-named. The only nuts to be found there were metal ones to screw around bolts. The 'Lane' and its bigger brother, Hunslet Road, had become highways to the engineering foundries which sprang up on sites from Leeds Bridge to Thwaite Gate on the city boundary. The two decades following were mushroom beds for heavy industry. From the back-to-back, privacy-destroying terraced houses that wove a tight herring-bone pattern around Hunslet Road, Hunslet Carr and Jack Lane, fitters, welders, turners, moulders, pattern-makers, smiths, and labourers converged down these main roads. The rhythmic clang of iron-shod clogs and boots rang out on the Yorkshire-stone pavements, as muffler-throated they made for the clocking-on boards of Kitsons, Fowlers, Hudswell Clarkes and many others sharing in this industrial boom south of the river. If T.S. Eliot had known Leeds as well as he knew London he might have substituted 'Leeds' for 'London' when he wrote

> *'Unreal city*
> *Under the brown fog of a winter dawn,*
> *A crowd flowed over London Bridge so many*
> *I had not thought death had undone so many.'*

And, north of the river, not to be outdone in this 'where there's muck there's money' business, Greenwood and Batley, Thomas Green, Fairbairns, and others were already successfully manufacturing. A great period not only for engineering but for a variety of industries which would help Leeds keep a good rate of employment if recession should gnaw at other less fortunate centres.

The housing pattern of Hunslet was duplicated in the Kirkstall Road district—a centre of leather manufacture—and its tightly packed residents must have taken a thoroughly 'familiarity breeds contempt' attitude to the ozone which encompassed them around. The local reporters, passing through the district said that 'the odours call up no sweet fancies about spices of Araby'. Passing the tannery on many occasions as a boy I could not have agreed more with those old-time journalists.

From the tannery it is probably a worthwhile thought to wash away the smell with a more wholesome one—the brewer's treatment of malt and hops. Inevitably, as a 'loiner' the primal thought is of *Tetley's Brewery*. Paradoxically we look first at one William Sykes. Not of course Nancy's Bill Sykes but the one who wrote:-

Mr WILLIAM SYKES, Common Brewer, returns his sincere Thanks for the Favours conferred on him by his numerous Friends during a Period of Thirty Years past, and begs to inform them, that in consequence of a determination to decline Business, he has Let his Brewery, and disposed of his Establishment to Mr JOSHUA TETLEY, whom he most respectfully recommends as his successor. Salem Place, Leeds, Oct 31, 1822.

which newspaper announcement immediately preceded

JOSHUA TETLEY informs the Public, that he has taken Mr SYKES'S BREWERY in Salem-Place, Hunslet-Lane and respectfully solicits a Continuance of those Favours, so long and so liberally conferred on his Predecessor. Joshua Tetley assures his friends, and the customers of Mr Sykes, that he has spared no expense in selecting the best MALT and HOPS, and in making Arrangements for carrying on the ALE and PORTER BREWING in such a Manner, as he trusts will meet their Approbation, and ensure their Patronage. A stock of the best South Country and other FLOUR always on Hand, in Parcels not less than a Sack; and MALT of the first quality, ready ground, in any Quantity, and on most reasonable Terms. Salem-Place, Hunslet-Lane, Leeds, October 31, 1822.

Tetley's was born: it began *brewing* in that post-Waterloo era but it is fair to say it was conceived out Armley way many decades previously. William Tetley, who started it all in 1746, became a maltster in a big way. It was his son **Joshua Tetley** who inserted the public notice and took over Skyes' premises in Salem Place. We associate monks with the production of wines and brewing for their own enjoyment, but Nonconformists are usually more readily linked with the Band of Hope movement. *Salem* Place however reminds us that the brewery and the Congregational chapel after which the street was named were good neighbours across a narrow street and that many a morning congregation had sung its praises strengthened by the rich and fruity odour wafting across. I am sure that when they sang W. G. Tarrant's

'Now praise we great and famous men
The fathers named in story'

they did not have Sykes or Tetley in mind. At least not more than a few of them.

Joshua was taking a chance. There had been a run of bad harvests, famines and Corn Laws—no doubt, the red lights of which Sykes had taken heed. But Joshua may have heard that 'if a man can write a better book, preach a better sermon, or make a better mouse-trap, than his neighbour, though he build his house in the woods, the world will make a beaten path to his door.' If so that could only mean one thing. Brew beer better than his competitors. Brewing from his own malt his position would be—and his beer *could* be—twice as strong. Whatever the workings of his mind on that last day of October 1822, Joshua Tetley took on the brewery, lock, stock, and barrel for £409 0s. 6d. Note the humble sixpence. Did those two Leeds worthies bargain over terms. Unmistakably. And in the manner of true Yorkshire thrift to which a Scot cannot hold a candle!

In those days it was the custom for the country and professional families, and many inns, to brew their own beer, which was bad for brewers generally but not quite so loss-making to Tetley who if he could not sell them 'bitter' could at least furnish them with malt. Building up the brewery, in spite of his dedication to quality, was hard. Twenty-six years after taking over his total workforce was only thirty-two men. Then, as we have seen, Hunslet, Holbeck, Kirkstall ....and Leeds surged forward to success. Heavy industry boomed almost overnight. The working men had their shillings in their pockets to spend and their employers 'non-Wilson' pounds with which to play. The brewery boomed in step with its neighbours. By 1856 he had more than doubled his staff—he now had a wage roll of over a hundred. He had lived to taste the fruits of success and when he died shortly afterwards, in 1859, he knew his brain-child would continue as a worthy successor to his father's Armley maltings.

Dad's Army may be television fiction but Joshua Tetley's grandsons could refer to Dad's Army as a fact. Until the Crimean War the standard weapon for an infantryman was a musket, but something with a more rapid rate of accurate fire was sought. The rifle was the answer but the Government of the day was also defence-cut minded and thought the cost to make these new weapons regulation issue would be prohibitive. Independent groups of public-spirited citizens banded together and in 1859 the Leeds Volunteers of Napoleonic times were reformed as the Leeds Rifles. Tetley's, from the boardroom to the malting floor, were filled with enthusiasm in spite of the stipulation of one guinea entrance free plus an annual subscription of two guineas. What is more, volunteers in the new regiment had to purchase their own uniforms and rifles. More than seventy men, led by Francis Tetley, still wanted to join and, as this was sufficient to form a company, No. 8 Company came into being—'Tetley's Own', the forerunner of part of a battalion of the West Yorkshire Regiment, when even the dray horses were taken on the company strength. When the Regiment finally became Artillery they were ideal for pulling gun-barrels as well as beer-barrels.

1862 saw the younger members of the family take another calculated risk based on an intuition that their reputation as brewers was riding on the crest of a wave. They gave up the sale of malt—customers would be able to buy only beer. Concurrent with this decision, the family purchased the freehold of the brewery land and an army of a different kind to No. 8 Company moved in—architects and artisans to erect malt stores, boiler houses, tall chimneys and barrel-washing sheds. Salem chapel was to have a bigger brother Tetley as neighbour and by the way business was booming in the '70s and '80s, a permanent neighbour. They tell in the firm that the boom really started the day great-grandson Charles came into it. Competitors were turning themselves into public limited companies in order to acquire capital to purchase public houses, with their ready made outlet for specialised sales. The Tetley family, although not owning one red brick of the 'Old Red Lions' of Leeds and its surrounds, resisted the temptation of easy public capital until 1897. Before lunch on the very first day of issue their Debentures (offering 3½% per annum!) were subscribed several times over.

We leave Tetley's at the turn of the century knowing that Joshua had founded a truly Yorkshire brewery, which twenty years ago joined its expertise to the expansive Allied Breweries.

One of the boundary roads of Tetley's is Crown Point Road and there a secular neighbour has a printing works not only of local renown but of international repute. Any tale of the city's leaders of industry would be incomplete without the 'Crown Point Story'; for who has not heard of **Alf Cooke's** or seen or read some of their handiwork. Like so many of the Hunslet 'giants' the firm's centenary has come and gone, for it was in 1866 that the twenty-four year old Alf founded yet another industrial dynasty.

Cooke was born in Leeds in 1842, the son of a shopkeeper in Meadow Lane. He sampled school life at the Collegiate Institute, Meanwood Lodge, and learnt the value of unquestioning obedience to one's seniors. In 1866 he marched confidently into matrimony and a business of his own. Annie Nickson from north Leeds was his bride and they raised three sons and seven daughters. Surrounded by a various assortment of traders—a boot and shoe maker, the Leeds Co-operative Flour Company, a grocer; and a post office, he laid out his counter with stationery and newspapers and put up a notice stating that he undertook letter-press printing. He prospered and within the remarkable short space of twelve months he had installed his first lithographic press. Two-horse trams clanked and clattered past his shop at a top speed of five miles per hour—slow enough for the passengers to mark and digest the presence of 'A. Cooke—Printer'. On foot top-hatted businessmen, bowler-hatted artisans and nondescript attired labourers accompanied by voluminously clad womenfolk, heads bonnetted or shawled according to the class division, jostled each other on the mud-splattered pavements. All possible customers as Alf worked and waited behind his counter and printing-press.

It was then the practice of shopkeepers to give Christmas gifts to favoured clientele. Cooke decided to print a pictorial almanac featuring Santa Claus and local tradesmen welcomed it with open arms. His inspiration netted him £70. It was not long after this Christmas that an unusual incident occurred. After banking hours he had popped cheques worth £90 through his bank's letter box, but passing next morning he found a crowd round a notice pinned to the door—'Bank closed'. He gained admittance by a side entrance and vehemently argued that, as the bank had not commenced business since he made his 'deposit', the money still legally belonged to him. He won his argument and the return of his cheques. He was, as he showed throughout his commercial life, a man of determination and purpose. Early in the 1870s he bought (he had previously been on a rental basis in Hunslet Road) premises near Crown Point Bridge and since then 'Crown Point' has been an integral part of his trade mark.

It seemed that fortune was prepared to smile on this energetic young family man, but in 1880 she turned her back on him. The Crown Point works were gutted by fire—totally destroyed. He must already have been well-esteemed, and his worth appreciated, because a local banker advanced him quite a considerable sum—thirty thousand pounds. He bought a new site on the west side of Hunslet Road; within a year the new factory was in operation and within four years the debt wiped off. Pertinacity was not the only outstanding quality of this thoroughly likeable and domesticated man, still on the right side of forty; his skill as a printer must have been considerable. In 1885 artist Sir Phillip Cunliffe-Owen, much impressed by the quality of Crown Point reproductions, secured him the royal warrant. When we analyse the award we realise it was an achievement extraordinary. On December 28th, Sir Phillip wrote 'that although the case did not come strictly within the conditions under which warrants were granted....Her Majesty has, under the circumstances, permitted that an exception shall be made in the present instance'. The entry in the *London Gazette* of January 5th, 1886, read:

> 'The exceptional position of Mr Alf Cooke is that he holds the one and only appointment of Chromo-Lithographer to Her Majesty the Queen in the entirety of Her Majesty's Dominions.'

Just twenty years after he had put up his simple notice in Hunslet Road. Giants' strides.

Although we are looking at leaders themselves, this I think can be an appropriate point to break from his personal success story and listen to a young boy, J. G. Pullen, who joined at the time of the royal warrant. He gives an authentic picture of conditions in those early days; a canvas showing an aspect of Leeds office life, resembling a page from a Victorian novel:

'All correspondence was carefully hand-written and shorthand writers—all male—were something of a mystery; indeed, Charlie Thompson, one of the first of them to be employed, was regarded by the rest of the staff as being definitely unusual. The office hours were long; usually recognised as a fifty-five hour week, though I rarely finished before eight o'clock, and often nine or ten. The office staff totalled eleven, all male. After about twelve months I decided to get a job in my native village of Idle, near Bradford, and having worked my notice I mounted my 'Penny farthing' bicycle and departed. Upon discovering conditions at my new firm were not going to be an improvement, I rode back to Crown Point and asked for my job back. Mr Cooke set me on again. I wonder how many would have done that.'

To revert to Alf's personal fortunes, it was incredible that a second disastrous fire could occur, but in September 1894 the factory was again reduced to a 'blackened and roofless shell...and indistinguishable wreckage'. What news to receive whilst on holiday at Scarborough.

How did this dogged Yorkshireman re-act. Firstly within ten days his workpeople were printing again in an old warehouse a few hundred yards away; secondly, he engaged a well-known architect to design a larger factory for the old site, with two tiers of galleries and extensive glass in the roof. Despite a severe winter and—yes, even in those days—a bricklayers' strike the new works were in production before the end of 1895. As an employer Alf was forthright but fair. I felt the current industrial scene could not have too many 'Cookes' when I learnt that he once received an ultimatum from his manager and chief clerk. Unless they received a share of the profits they would leave. They left!

Whilst the idea of profit-sharing was frowned upon, he offered weekly bonuses to keep machinery and factory floor clean. There is no doubt though that factory life, by comparison with modern conditions, was severe—the working day began at 7.0 a.m. and finished at 5.30 p.m...and they worked on Saturday mornings. Discipline was maintained by a series of fines for late arrival, smoking, riding on the hoists, stopped machines before time. Fines ranged from twopence to a shilling. When being put on the payroll the employee had to read the Rule Book he had introduced, the preface of which read, 'Any person who objects to work under these rules can give in his or her notice to leave'.

He called 'a spade a spade' and not an instrument on which to lean and meditate, but nevertheless he was regarded as a model employer and the father of many of the better conditions to be later enjoyed in the printing trade. But on what note to conclude the story of this remarkable Hunslet lad? I like the news I was given of his concern at the Leeds housewives being unjustly exploited in the 1880s by local fishmongers. By way of exposure he bought two Scarborough fishing boats and renamed them *Crown Point I* and *Crown Point II*. 'From net to customer' was his fishing motto and he retailed his catches in a large marquee in the Black Bull field behind the works. It was an outstanding success. Hundreds of women walked long distances to buy fish at three-halfpence—about ½p—a pound..... and that was 50 per cent less than local shop prices.

Nineteenth century entrepreneur and pioneer printer with the royal warrant, he used his many talents without regard for orthodoxy and attacked injustices with ceaseless vigour. He died at the age of sixty and in the following year the firm was registered as a private limited company to continue its progress to the present day. We will leave the printing works at the extensions which were built on the site formerly occupied by St Jude's church, a little further down Hunslet Road. There the 1960 Board of Directors thoughtfully incorporated into one of the windows of the new building the centre section of the former east window of the church. Beneath it stands a plaque which reads,

'IN MEMORIAM. This extension to our works was added in 1962. It occupies the site of St Jude's Church which was built in 1853. Due to the gradual exodus of its congregation to the outskirts of the city, this church ultimately fell into disuse and thus in 1954 was deconsecreated and finally demolished. This section of the east window of the church which you see marks its site for perpetuity.'

In the second half of the nineteenth century the printing industry was growing rapidly and nowhere faster than Leeds. In 1851 the city had 42 printing firms with a workforce of 800; by the end of the century there were 170 firms with 7,000 employees. We have remembered Alf Cooke who took part in the early stages of this boom, and as it is not a long step from Crown Point Road to Thwaite Gate it seemed timely to look at a firm created at the *end* of this expansive period. We go down Hunslet Road, past the junction where Hunslet Carr hives off to the right and take the right hand fork to Wakefield. At the bottom of Belle Hill, the now familiar buildings of **John Waddington Ltd** where we will ask about.....no, not John Waddington but the real 'Mr Waddington'. The first question usually asked at John Waddington's is 'Who was John Waddington and what connection had he with the firm?'

The answer is simple; he gave his name to the company and that is about all. Waddington started just after the turn of the century, mainly printing posters for the theatrical world. By 1913 his firm was deeply in debt and the decision to close down was imminent, when the foreman persuaded the powers that be to let him try to revive the business with its 23 employees and worth......*minus* £10,000.

By the twenties Waddingtons were successful. We ask our second question, 'Who was the magus who picked up the pieces and created a new edifice that for sixty years now has been pre-eminent in a specialised field of printing?' Again a simple reply.......... **Victor H. Watson**.

Victor was born near Kennington Oval—does that explain his great love of cricket or was that a Yorkshire graft that bore fruit?—in 1878 as one of thirteen children to parents living in humble circumstances. At a very early age his parents moved to Leeds, so he only missed the title of 'loiner' by a whisker. He left school at the age of twelve and two years later he had become apprenticed to Goodall and Suddick, another of the old Leeds names in the world of printing. After serving his time, he joined Harrison Townend as a lithographer and his apprentice days with a progressive firm enabled him to take full advantage of their keenness to keep abreast of the latest trade developments. In 1907 his brother-in-law, a lithographic artist, had persuaded him to apply to John Waddingtons for the job of lithographic foreman. Victor had personality, enthusiasm for his work and unbounded energy. With a handful of these trumps he could not help but make his presence felt. He not only improved the quality of the printing but he had the old-fashioned habit of exceeding what was asked of him. Another who had the ball at his feet and was not afraid to shoot hard. He was not asked or expected to secure business for the company but he did and in no small measure. Watson's additional orders increased the turnover by a third!

Some years later Victor told in his own words of the watershed in the company's life. I quote verbatim:- 'I asked for and was given by the Directors six months to put the Company on its feet and that if at the end of this time the position had not improved, the firm would be closed down. It was even difficult to pay the first week's wages, suppliers would not send goods without cash and there were a number of customers who could be classed as extremely doubtful payers. I persuaded my main supplier of paper and my main supplier of printing ink to allow six months credit. At the same time I was fortunate enough to obtain a substantial order for a magazine and received payment for this work in advance.'

He spent much time and effort looking for ways to increase business. He noticed that many successful firms had specialities which called for high quality work. A keen card-player, it seemed to him that playing cards would be ideal for his purpose. His decision to manufacture these was the lifebelt for himself and his fellow passengers on what had looked a sinking ship. He recognised the far-reaching effects of the photo-offset printing process, took full advantage of this method, and soon influenced the way in which the industry evolved. Unfortunately, in the thirties, Waddington shared in the general trade recession and again business was on an ebb tide. Two factories came to the rescue. The tobacco combine, W.D. & H.O. Wills, brought out their playing card scheme and with it the need for large quantities of first rate packs. Victor was not slow to become involved and Waddingtons supplied on a grand scale.

Contemporary with this windfall he introduced 'Lexicon', a family game which proved a winner. The tide turned again and, whilst no printing firm could ever be said to have a monopoly of business, eventually Victor Watson's inventive company achieved the impossible—they had 'Monopoly', that family circle card, dice and board game that was to bring lasting fame. I don't think that for one moment that the boy from Kennington Oval ever dreamt that by the end of the 1970s the public address system at Liverpool Street station would echo with the words: 'The next train leaving platform eight will be the 10.45 'Monopoly' Express to King's Cross, calling at Fenchurch Street. All passengers wishing to go to Gaol, please take their seats.' The 1979 British Monopoly championships were under way, with the heats being played on a train and finals in London Dungeon, a museum that has been created in the arches under the London Bridge station. His successors could not obtain permission for Armley (or any other) gaol so opted for a substitute!

Douglas Brearley, a retired director, told me that as a man Victor H. Watson was a loveable character, who expected and received complete loyalty in return. He was fully cognisant of his debt to his colleagues saying of them, 'The fact that I have been lucky in finding the right men has contributed largely to the success of the firm—it is absolutely essential that the heads of firms should have this gift if they are going to make a success of the business they are in control of, simply because the amount of work it is possible for one man to do is limited.' His recognition of character and their future potentialities can be no better illustrated than by the fact that he named his son Eric Winston after Winston Churchill....long before World War I and long before Churchill had made his mark on British and world history.

A family man, he was also passionately fond of music, particularly the light operas of Gilbert and Sullivan. So far as cricket was concerned he was as fanatical as any indigenous Yorkshireman. The small cricket ground almost surrounded by the Wakefield Road factory is his memorial. He persuaded a famous cricket-groundsman to lay out the wicket. Another more orthodox memorial, the family gravestone, has the inscription 'Nothing is denied well directed energy'. A fitting summary of his life which ended in 1943, following a heart attack believed to have been hastened by the accumulation of war-time worries and frustrations, and his deep concern for his son Eric fighting in North Africa.

Victor Watson has brought us near enough the present day to hand on the torch of 'Leader of Industry' to a 'loiner' bred and born, with whom it was my privilege to share the same school form-room many years ago; one who rose to head one of the world's largest business empires with annual sales of £3½ billion, employing

340,000 people in 70 countries; a man who headed a Government commission to decide on the pay packet of every doctor and dentist in the land; and now a retired gentleman, honoured by a knighthood, who can look back on a life of satisfaction and fun in a continuous process of learning—**Sir Ernest Woodroofe**.

Ernest George Woodroofe was born on 6th January 1912 in the Domestic Street area of Holbeck, the son of the office manager of a railway goods station in the heart of the city. He realised early in his educational life that success would depend on his own efforts. When he was at his primary school—a small church school flanked by the ever present rhubarb fields of the locality—his father warned him, 'I can see you through secondary school, but I can't afford to get you through the university. For that you'll have to get scholarships.'

His first target in life was clear. Why not make a start on this scholarship business and also save Dad the secondary school fees? His very small school gave scholarship candidates special tuition in the boiler-house. He took full advantage and was awarded an entry to Cockburn High School in Burton Road, off Dewsbury Road, a red-brick, no-nonsense centre of learning with a blue riband of successes for would-be university undergraduates. It was there his development still remains clearly focussed in my mind. Our tutors were dedicated to their task of seeing that each one of the forty-eight boys and girls (yes, co-educational even in those days of the twenties) who comprised the matriculation class passed with flying colours. That meant the aim was to secure at least a 60% mark simultaneously in eight subjects. Matriculation in the twenties was a 'sudden death' affair—one failure below 60% and the whole certificate was forfeited. It must have been a Cockburn master who coined the phrase 'Gone for a Burton'. The teaching staff included such men and women as 'Boz' Milner, 'Billy' Peaker, 'Ma' Hampton and C.L. Champion, B.Sc. 'C.L.' will be forever associated with those degree initials 'B.Sc.' I can never think of him without that appendage and I think it is a psychological quirk paying a subconscious tribute to the excellence of his teaching and mastery of physics. It is no mere coincidence that Ernest Woodroofe, looking back and telling us that he was naturally inclined towards science, went for physics. Why? 'Because the physics master was not only a first rate teacher and man but a damned good cricketer, and like the rest of the school I idolized him.'

Woodroofe, with his 'Harold Lloyd' spectacles of those days, a quiff of black hair which was constantly straying onto his forehead, and which, along with his glasses, was forever being pushed up with his fingers, cycled quite a distance each day to Cockburn and a football match on a games afternoon meant four cycle trips that day. He was called upon to make the quadruple journey regularly because he was as good a soccer full-back as he was a scholar. He was the school team's defensive cover to a goalkeeper who did not make his mark at Elland Road but at the B.B.C.—Jack Singleton, producer of the 'Two of a Kind' programme.

Ernest Woodroofe achieved his target of Leeds University and turned over in his mind possible careers. 'I thought about being a teacher, even more I thought about being a surgeon, but put that out of my head—I knew money would be required to become a surgeon. And it just wasn't there.' He began thinking about industry, especially after two years research on atomic physics and saw himself as an industrial researcher. They gave him a 'first' and then his Doctorate of Philosophy.

The introduction in 1935 to Unilever came about by chance when, just after the slump, jobs were hard to come by. His university professor had a cousin there and he joined the seed-crushing and oil-refinery plant at Silvertown in London's East End. For a year he was employed doing all manner of odd development work, some in the laboratory, some out in the factory. It was then he first realised that the education he really needed was in chemical engineering, which he proceeded to study in his spare time. He also discovered that his knowledge of the chemistry of oils and fats was rudimentary, so he was not averse to attending evening classes at Regent Street Polytechnic. As a good Yorkshireman he discovered that he was not earning enough money and to put this right he became a lecturer in mathematics at Woolwich Polytechnic. Busy as a beaver, taking lectures at one Polytechnic, giving lectures at another, studying chemical engineering in his 'digs', and during the day making all manner of studies in the factory. In his own words 'as happy as a sandboy' until he found he knew *nothing* about accountancy, so, of course this subject must be added to his other activities.

He was then asked to take over as transport manager—'yard manager' they termed it at the time. One of Sir Ernest's favourite aphorisms regarding industrial life is linked with the cobbler and his last. Not *sticking* to the last, as is usually indicated, but *moving away* from it for wider expansion; trying one's hand in other spheres. Following his position in transport he certainly sampled variety. Departmental factory manager, back to technology and chemical engineering, manager of a single factory, then a group of factories and in 1949 a lengthy course at Harvard Business School on the Advanced Management Programme. I liked his aside, 'My fellow students had two very good names for us older students. Some called us "re-treads" and others preferred "pot-bellied executives"'. By leaving his last the 'cobbler' was being groomed for stardom. He was soon marked out to be head of Unilever Research—the pace of success was quickening, an exciting time in his career. From head of research to vice-chairman and then, in the seventies, the ultimate appointment, chairman of the company.

When he took office Unilever was the tenth largest company in the world and the second biggest outside America. His predecessor, Lord Cole, once said, 'Firms are often compared to ships. Well, Unilever isn't a ship; it's a fleet—several different fleets, several hundred subsidiary companies—and the ships many different sizes, doing all kinds of different things, all over the place'. A gigantic grocer's shop—a hypermarket—with 300 senior managers at the head of several hundred different operating units in 70 different countries. And the boy from Holbeck who cycled daily to Dewsbury Road and booted a hefty ball for his school down Parkside way was the man in charge. The far reaching decisions which affect the lives of all those thousands of workers—and millions of customers, too—were, after studying and consulting with senior colleagues, his to make. Why did a lad from a humble background reach such eminence? We have seen the broad framework but let him show us one or two of the nuts and bolts as he tells of episodes that he labels 'breakthroughs'.

'There were five factories in Scotland, two of them in bad shape, unproductive, losing money, heading for closing down. I was put in charge of those five factories. The director in charge of the whole of our activities in the area sent for me and said—I was thirty-two at the time—"You've got a better brain than I have, and you've had a better training. Here's your opportunity. Get on with it. Pull this business through if you can. Make the decisions. If they're the wrong ones I'll tick you off, but out behind the scenes; out front I'll back you all the way. Don't forget I've been trading all my life. I know far more about the business than you do. Come to me if you want advice. Off you go!"

'Men like that are worth their weight in gold and I am eternally grateful for the training he gave me. Well, I slogged away. One of the factories was a very tough spot, in the middle of a shipbuilding area where in those days the men were difficult to work with. The machinery was always breaking down, usually in the middle of the night. I used to go back into the factory myself and personally supervise getting the plant back into running order. There were far too many men there, and working inefficiently. Costs were killing the place. I had to lay men off. I wasn't always popular. I recall being told one day I would find myself strung up on a lamp-post! But it was thin out, or close down, and gradually the workers came to face it. Then, when they saw the place was pulling around, they began to take an interest, began to co-operate, and get better results. I had showed them when they were bottom of the league table of performance. I showed them when they were halfway up. Then came a day when we got a letter from the chairman of the company in London. He said "I congratulate you all on your results." It was a red-letter day.'

His next breakthrough he feels would be better described as a 'break'. 'The head of research for Unilever resigned—he didn't see eye to eye with the chairman and the board. They were not satisfied that research had sufficiently related to the practical needs of the business. So in effect they said: "Is there anybody in the company who understands business and also has some understanding of scientific research?" They looked around and gave me the job. No one was more surprised than me!'

Looking back, he indicated that a major fascination of holding the reins had been the power to change things, the power not to have to accept things as they are. He referred to increasing efficiency and productivity by re-organising the running of a factory, substituting antiquated machinery with modern equipment. To the wonderful feeling of having done something; of not being the slave of conditions around him; of the feeling of freedom, of human accomplishment. He summed this up as 'the power to change, to dominate self and environment by will and intelligence, is what being human is about'.

But from the high pinnacle he was still very much a family man. His first wife, a Leeds girl from his own Holbeck environment, died of cancer in 1961. He met his second wife, an Oxford graduate, when the Oxford Appointments Committee recommended Unilever to her and she became Sir Ernest's secretary. As he phrases it, 'I got a bonus out of our recruiting efforts!' With his wife he shares a love of travel and foreign dishes. He is occasionally in the kitchen trying his hand with research there. The 'cobbler' again! He also admits to a spot of wood-carving in his earlier days and has returned to this first love in retirement. He has helped shape Unilever and says there is lots of satisfaction in 'shaping a bit of wood to his own fancy'.

'Have you any message to pass on to a young man of today?'

'My sentiments throughout life haven't really changed. I still think that one ingredient necessary for success is the attitude that education must continue throughout one's career. I still think that one mustn't be too concerned about sticking to one's last. I admire ambition in young people, but ambition is best satisfied by doing one's current job enthusiastically, thoroughly and with distinction.'

'With distinction.' I was back with him, in memory, when those 1928 matriculation results came through to Cockburn School. There were several distinctions against Woodroofe, E.G.'s name.

One final question to him. 'Any other profession you would like to have followed if not that of an industrialist?'

'A surgeon: the satisfaction of changing something, of saving life, releasing somebody from pain, using manipulative skill to make order and life when there was mess and disease. Yes, a surgeon. But I am happy and fulfilled having done what I have.'

2. Great Traders

Michael Marks (Marks and Spencer) — Snowden Schofield — Montague Burton — Robert Barr (Wallace Arnold)

FROM Beeston and Burmantofts; from Roundhay and Rothwell; wherever Mr Leeds and his wife lived in the days when the trams were the city's main form of mass transportation, they almost invariably met each other and their friends at the spot that seemed to have become by tradition the only meeting place in town ..... 'Dyson's'. Just after lunch on winter Saturdays the church football teams, and the local rugger clubs, assembled their players; just after lunch on summer Saturdays, the bag-carrier of the cricket elevens stood as a marker, around whom the batsmen and the bowlers would gather; cycling clubs, and rambling clubs; scout troops and guide companies going to be 'happy when they're hiking' across Adel Moor or Ilkley Moor; on every Saturday, winter or summer, husbands met wives for a shopping expedition; fiancés met fiancées for a courting expedition.....the great outdoor movement met at.... 'Dyson's'. Under the clock, but if the trams from Dewsbury Road and Balm Road in the south, and from Meanwood Road and Compton Road in the north, disgorged too many for the pavement outside 'Dyson's' then next door, 'Hardy's', took the overspill. 'Dyson's', not a big firm by shop-floor space, but jewellers of merit; 'Hardy's', not a Harrods by any means, though gent's outfitters of taste; two stalwarts—one happily still with us—of Briggate, the centre of the city's traders from way back in 1258 when probably a dozen stalls were the forebears of the supermarkets of today.

In looking at great traders of Leeds there can be no better starting point than Briggate, which houses a store known throughout the land and which all began a stone's throw away in Kirkgate Market. St. George for England but St. Michael for Leeds!

St. Michael, the brand name of **Marks and Spencer**, is one of the best known in the world today. In Britain, over 13 million customers in more than 250 stores every week, spending about £1,700 million on food, clothing and house furnishings. It is scarcely an exaggeration to say everybody shops at Marks and Spencer. The staff at the great store near Marble Arch in London are quite accustomed to serving Princess Anne and Princess Alexandra with underwear; visiting Arabs (officially forbidden to enter a Jewish shop) spend thousands of pounds on a single shopping spree; day excursionists come from Hamburg and other European cities for an afternoon's shopping at 'M & S'. And it all began on a trestle table in Kirkgate Market in 1884.

To trace the real background story of that unbelievable insignificant conception we must go still further back in time. **Michael Marks**, the founder of the firm, was born in 1863 at Bialystock, a village in what was then Russian Poland. He was the youngest of his family and, his mother having died in childbirth, he was brought up by his eldest sister. His father is said to have been employed in the timber trade but when Michael was married he described his father's occupation as a tailor. We know little of his childhood and youth, except that he and his family shared the poverty and hardship to which the great majority of the Jews of Poland and Russia were condemned. To these afflictions were added social and political disabilities; they constituted an inferior stratum of the population and formed a community of their own founded on suffering and oppression. The fact is important in the life of Marks and his children because it left them with a deep consciousness of the ill-treatment of Jews and the hope that one day they might be able to compensate in some small way. If there was any relief for the Jews from the harshness of their conditions it was to be found in a religious faith, and a pride in their race and history, to which they clung all the more assiduously because of the injustices; and in the warmth and intimacy of the human relationships within their closed community. In 1881 their severity of life was intensified by the assassination of Tsar Alexander II and the violent outbreaks of anti-semitism which followed. The Jews responded with a wave of immigration. Among the millions of immigrants were many who themselves or through their descendants have made outstanding contributions to every aspect of life to their adopted countries. Michael Marks was one of these men.

We do not know the exact year in which he emigrated but it would appear to have been not later than 1882 when he was 19 years old. He arrived with few advantages except his inbuilt abilities; he had no money; he had not been trained in any trade; he knew no English, neither could he read or write. On arrival he found that the one source to which he might have looked for help had eluded him. His brother Barnet had left earlier for England but when Michael arrived his brother had continued his wanderings to America, having been attracted by the Gold Rush to the Yukon.

But our young Marks had the knack of making and keeping friends, a trait that helped him tremendously throughout life.

Like most Jews, he went first to London then moved to Leeds. From then onwards the North was to be the mainspring of his activities. He chose Leeds, no doubt, because the city had already a Jewish community of six to seven thousand folk concentrated in the area known as the 'Leylands' and mostly employed in the rapidly developing clothing trade. It was an occupation not requiring a high degree of training or skill and he could be fairly sure of finding work and help amongst fellow refugees. That was the backcloth to his coming to Leeds.

At this time the city was rapidly expanding, with a population of just over 300,000; it was a railway centre and a hub for clothing manufacturers with more than its share of heavy and mining industries. Typical of the newly emergent industrial Britain, with a large working class section relishing an income which had risen in real terms. The increasing demand for domestic articles was a natural outcome and parallel with it was the ability to cope at a reasonable selling price because of growing mass production. In the previous decade departmental stores, too, had sprung up, to cater for the now prosperous middle classes. A good business man, with the acumen to accurately assess the wants and tastes of his customers, searching for fertile soil in which to plant new ideas, need look no further than Leeds.

Into this scene walked the men to match the time and the place, with fate, as repeatedly happens, weaving the threads into a soon-to-be discernible pattern. At No. 32, Kirkgate was a wholesale merchant's firm, I.J. Dewhirst Ltd., who had built up a business supplying pedlars with their wares. Isaac Dewhirst was walking down Kirkgate when a stranger stopped him and spoke the single word 'Barrans'. It soon became clear to Dewhirst that the man spoke no English other than this word 'Barrans', and he assumed that he was looking for the clothing firm of that name. He remembered his manager, Charlie Backhouse, spoke a little Yiddish and could perhaps ascertain just what this pleasant Jewish fellow needed. He took him to his office where it was confirmed that he had come to find Barran's clothing factory—John Barran's readiness to give work to Jewish refugees was known in Poland and to take the one word 'Barrans' to Leeds was a password to comparative security. Isaac was fascinated by the stranger; small in stature but with a personality that shone through his poverty and lack of knowledge of English. He offered him a loan of five pounds to tide him over the immediate future, little realising that the offer of that loan was the minute grain of seed from which the gigantic 'M & S' would ultimately blossom. Michael Marks, the stranger, looking round the pedlar's warehouse, asked if he might use the loan to buy goods. It was agreed and as the debt was repaid, instalment by instalment, Michael was allowed to take away further goods. A pedlar's life in any generation was never easy. At that time and in a Yorkshire climate, for a foreigner of frail physique it was hard graft. His aim was to replace door-to-door peddling as soon as he could with a fixed site and he had his eye on a market stall in Kirkgate; the nearer his benefactor, the more secure he would feel. He took a chance, and so in 1884 he put up his trestle table in the Kirkgate open market and traded on the only possible days—Tuesdays and Saturdays. Obviously this was not sufficient to earn him a living so he took his trestle and his wares to Castleford and Wakefield, towns that had markets on other days. When he had to leave his Leeds stall to buy more merchandise at Dewhirsts, Charlie Backhouse came across the road and stood in for him. It is amazing that the link between Marks and Spencers and Dewhirsts has never been broken. They still are suppliers to the giant emporium of our time.

Business prospered. From the open market he moved to the covered market, dividing his stall into two sections. Originally he displayed his merchandise in open baskets, with price tickets clearly showing his customers the cost, and allowing them to handle and inspect the goods. But a luminous flash and his stall (and later his shops) had a unique character. He classified his articles according to price and placed all those costing a penny in one section and all those costing more in the other, with price tags. Above the penny section he hung a board with the slogan 'Don't ask the price; it's a penny.' It proved one of the most successful advertising phrases ever invented. Striking in its simplicity, corresponding to a genuine popular need, it was inevitable that he adopted the principle of the fixed price for all his future trading. Henceforth he charged no more than a penny for everything he sold. Marks Penny Bazaar was off the ground.

Covering a wide range of haberdashery, hardware, household goods, soap, stationery and toys, the penny limit meant that he had to accept a *very* low profit margin. Reels of cotton at eleven shillings a gross and sold at a penny each gives some idea of the meagre return but it was a winning formula. Not only was his head full of ideas but it was also full of figures. He preferred mental arithmetic and never kept any accounts—in the event, his cash and carry basis with Dewhirsts made book work unnecessary.

He was launched in business and two years later into matrimony. In 1886 he married 21 year old Hannah Cohen at Belgrave Synagogue, and laid the foundation stone of a particularly happy married life. From that time on, his two main interests in life were his business and his home. His son Simon (later Lord Marks) was born in 1888 and his daughter Rebecca two years later.

Six years after the first trestle table he had five Penny Bazaars, having extended from his three West Riding towns to Warrington and Birkenhead. By now assistants had been appointed and he was looking for locations for further expansion in the market halls of

Yorkshire and Lancashire. 1891 saw a major change in his organisation. For the convenience of centrally-operating headquarters he moved to Wigan, opned in the market hall and set up his family in Caroline Street. His Manchester bazaar followed in 1894 and by then he realised that his business had become too large for one man to handle; he needed a partner.

His obvious preference was Isaac Dewhirst who had been a sheet anchor for ten years and who had continued to take an interest in young Michael's progress. He approached him with his suggestion but the offer was declined after consideration, the deciding factor being that Dewhirst Ltd. was extremely prosperous and the senior man had no desire for further commitments. He did, however, suggest that Thomas Spencer, his cashier and excellent book-keeper, might be interested and that he would have no objection to releasing him if he wished to avail himself of the opportunity.

Different in physique and temperament but with a common quality of kindness and consideration for others, Michael Marks and Thomas Spencer developed a friendship. Spencer was a burly man, fond of good food and liquor, authoritative but a first class organiser. He grasped the chance offered and on 28th September 1894 a partnership came into being with the ex-cashier paying £300 for a half share and the total capital stading at £450. With these two at the helm, failure was impossible and success inevitable. By 1903, forty bazaars had been created, the partners had formed a limited company and immediately afterwards Spencer retired, his small investment having multiplied fifty times. He only lived a further two years and two years later Michael died.

It was said of him that no more hardworking immigrant had ever found a niche in Leeds; his honesty, friendliness, sympathetic nature allied to business simplicity and directness meant he never throughout his life lost a friend. Marks and Spencer's reputation of 'value for money' can be traced back to its source—Michael Marks from Bialystock.

The company, after his death, was jointly owned by the sons of the original partners but neither was in a position to run the business. Simon Marks was only nineteen years of age and Thomas Spencer junior had no inclination to take on the responsibilities. Control passed to Spencer senior's executor and after several years of disagreement and wrangling as to how the firm should be run, Leeds-born Simon took control in 1917 to become chairman at the age of twenty-eight—a position he fulfilled until his death in 1964 having been created a baron three years earlier. Simon built on his father's solid foundation and steered 'M & S' into the modern era of High Street supermarkets to earn the title of 'the greatest merchant prince England has ever produced'. He worked closely with his brother-in-law, the late Lord Sieff, whom he had met at school in 1901 and on this almost lifelong friendship a unique partnership was created.

The private company became public in 1926, about the time when the original penny bargains had reached their fixed selling price of five shillings. Simon held this early policy of low prices for goods of high quality until the 1940s when it was inevitable that the price limit had to be abandoned. The St Michael label was the brainchild of Simon who decided that a trade name was long overdue. 'Michael' is of course derived from his father's name and the 'St' added from the St Margaret's goods with which the firm were then associated. Marks and Spencer could, during this period, have been equally appropriately named Marks and Sieff but it had become a British tradition in the rhyming slang of 'Marks and Sparks', and along with 'St Michael' this was registered as a trade name.

Not only was Simon Marks a great trader but, remembering the tales related by his father of his Jewish forbears in Russian Poland, he was a sincere and practical friend of his race, working towards a Jewish state in Palestine. As a multi-millionaire he was renowned for his philanthropy, and especially fond of medical charities and medical research. In addition to the honour which the Queen bestowed upon him, the medical world conferred a rare honour when in 1958 he was made an honorary Fellow of the Royal College of Surgeons. He was proud that he was one of only four laymen to be so honoured.

As 'St Michael' sails on beyond our shores—Belgium, France and Canada now know his sign—we leave our memories of the founder, and his son, in the Briggate store of to-day, so near to the old trestle table where you had no need to ask the price.

Having returned to Dyson's what next? I recalled again the trams with their tightly packed standing passengers. There was one wag of a conductor who was accustomed to shout, especially in January—'Hurry along, for Hitchen's Sale'. If it was not January then he would omit the word 'Sale', because at any season of the year 'Hitchen's' was a familiar name. Clarence Hitchen's haberdashery and ladies-wear emporium in Briggate was an old favourite but no longer with us. Try a little further along, near the former Empire Theatre. Matthias Robinson's, another shop to delight the feminine eye. Gone? I'm afraid so. What about Smith Bros? Another grand family firm that is but a memory. Leave Briggate and turn left at its junction with the Headrow, the wide artery cutting across the city centre from east to west. Here is the City Varieties, which has seen so many old time music-hall stars and is still captivating an even larger audience with its television sponsored 'Those were the days'. There is hope, perhaps that in this vicinity we might find a Leeds trader also with a history. Of course .... **Schofields.** Not many yards past the shy, almost camouflaged entrance of the City Varieties remains a monument to private enterprise, a departmental store with a well-known name for more than three-quarters of a century.

Bradford and Leeds, with only nine built-up miles separating them, are entirely different worlds to those born there. Different Yorkshire dialects; different trading habits; different holiday preferences between Morecambe and Scarborough. It would seem almost sacrilege to some old Leeds die-hards to include in a volume of this nature the story of a Bradford-born man but when we listen to the present chairman of Schofields, Peter Schofield, son of the founder, tell of his father's creating a business that is still expanding, then 'loiners' must bow to the inevitable. *Snowden Schofield's success story is a must.*

It was just a year after the turn of the twentieth century that Snowden, born in 1870, came to Leeds with £300 in his pocket and a fund of business experience accumulated in his native town, London and Liverpool. His family recall how chance played no small part in his destiny, because he had been much attracted by the idea of establishing a business in Blackburn when a small two-windowed shop became available in the recently opened Victoria Arcade. To the uninitiated it was an inconspicuous set of premises in an under-developed trading quarter of the city but to young Schofield it was an advantageous position in what could become a prestigious site. His judgement proved correct.....its situation became the cornerstone of the business that was quickly to acquire a reputation for quality.

1901, not only Schofield's year of decision but a momentous year for England. Queen Victoria had died—an epoch had ended; the Boer War dragged on; but the people stepped into the Edwardian era, full of optimistic enthusiasm; Britain was still mistress of the seas and the Empire was still one on which the sun never set. Schofield opened his shop with three assistants on the first Saturday in May. His first cash book revealed that on that opening day his takings were £62 3s 4½d—and £43 10s was in gold. He told his sons that it was a beautiful summer-like day and that his shop was packed from morning until the time he pulled down the blinds. It is more than nostalgic, it is fascinating to think of that robust chink on the counter of gold coins. Snowden told how in those first few days he remembered that the ladies drifted elegantly in and out of the shop in waistcoats and high collars, skirts and frocks bellowing, shod in buttoned boots, and adorned with flat straw hats. Some had left husbands, frock-coated and top-hatted, in Upperheadrow, waiting in their carriages. Horse omnibuses had brought his less well-to-do customers to see what this new shop in town was offering in opening bargains.

'When I opened', said Snowden Schofield, 'Irving was playing at the "Grand" and just down Albion Street you could buy half-a-dozen oysters and a pint of stout for a shilling [My goodness! my Guinness! ...yes, indeed]. Not only that but 3d. [the *old* threepence] would buy a man his fill of sausage and mash, and 2d. his pint of beer.'

This was the Leeds where a Bradfordian had the courage, the foresight, and the enthusiasm to conquer the ladies with his laces and ribbons, his furbelows and flounces. From the outset he proved that he had no intention of being just another shopkeeper....he was not to be a mere 'corner-shop'. He had ideas, and he was a practical psychologist. He said, looking back, 'All women were, and are, interested in pretty things. I set out to supply them in abundance and added companionship and service, for good measure. I wanted to transform shopping from something that was merely necessary into a real pleasure. I regarded it as a point of honour that no transaction in my shop was complete until my customer was completely satisfied.'

Snowden Schofield continued, according to his son, 'I am prepared to assert that the old fashioned copy-book maxims, like "Honesty is the best policy", still provide the soundest foundation for success in the commercial life. My recipe for success is simply "Do unto others as you would be done by". With these ideas well planted in his mind he started business in his little shop at a time when 'rich and poor bought plain black or ribbed woollen hose at 6¾d or at the most one and sixpence; when it did not matter if a stocking fitted a shapely leg, and footwear was a secondary consideration among the fair sex'.

No. 1, Victoria Arcade began to thrive. In only two years, business was so good that when No. 4 became vacant it was taken over for extensions. The still young principal was a pioneer in the use of publicity; letters, posters, handbills, catalogues. He tried them all but settled for press advertising—there is no doubt that today television commercials would have backed up his press campaigns. The use of the local press was, indeed, unusual because up to that time, quack medicines were the only things offered in the popular press, and at first his wanting to buy space on the front page for display advertising was rather frowned upon by the editorial staff. But his idea proved successful and looking back on that revolutionary step he said, 'We first advertised what was a huge quantity of nappa gloves. There were several hundreds of pairs, and we bought them for 1s. a pair and sold them at 1s 0¾d. We told the public about them in an advertisement four inches deep across two columns. We sold every pair in three days. Nevertheless it required courage and faith to continue, because the public were not used to seeing drapery advertised in that manner and probably thought it was not absolutely genuine. We succeeded by keeping our promises to the public and never exaggerating. They soon realised that the newspaper was our biggest shopwindow.'

In 1908, the year when both men and women were wearing straw boaters at 3s 6d each, and women's skirts sent little clouds billowing along the streets, business boomed so briskly that another shop was opened on the opposite end of the Arcade. In 1911 another advance was made with the purchase of the old Red Hall whose gabled roof was known to every Leeds citizen, and to Charles I. Schofield knew the part the house had played in history and treated it with due respect. He turned the King's Chamber, where Harrison had been received, into a fully equipped restaurant, whilst retaining all its characteristics. Oak wainscoting and ancient plaster work was preserved or restored.

After World War I, and now beyond fifty years of age, he began to delegate some of his responsibilities but still worked hard and never lost the gift of making other people give of their best. His captivating smile worked wonders with his staff and a welfare service underlined this concern for them.

As he grew in years and stature he gave freely of his best in almost every branch of the city's public life. The opening of the '30s decade—when Yorkshire's Amy Johnson was in the midst of her epic solo flight to Australia—saw his largest extension yet and almost doubled his ground floor space. Guildford Street, Upperheadrow and Lowerheadrow now made way for The Headrow and the Schofield store stood on one of the stateliest thoroughfares in the North of England. But it was still adjacent to a bit of the romantic past and this too was absorbed into his domain. Leeds Hippodrome, closed as a theatre in 1933 after a history stretching back nearly a hundred years, became part of Schofields in 1934. You might now buy your evening gown on the very spot where Vesta Tilley and Marie Lloyd had twice nightly changed into their theatrical costumes. In more recent times, Snowden's successors have taken over the Theatre Royal where Gladys Stanley flashed her shapely Principal Boy's tights in Francis Laidler's annual Christmas pantomimes.

One of the stumbling blocks obstructing his dream was a small tavern, the Cock and Bottle, that would persist in continuing to trade and cut in two his ever growing store. In 1938 it came on the market and quickly it was fitted in as another piece of a jigsaw puzzle which, bit by bit, was being fashioned into a modern super-emporium. Yet to what man proposes there often comes a time when larger happenings call an unexpected half. Chamberlain's scrap of paper had meant nothing. We were at war with Hitler and the Schofield ideals pigeon-holed. But the uneasy peace under the shadow of the atom bomb came and in 1947 Snowden Schofield bought Victoria Arcade—he now owned the entire site.

Two years later, on 24th March, Snowden Schofield died. He had seen his one shop grow until it filled a huge slice of Leeds' 'Golden Square Mile'. He had watched his staff expand from three to almost seven hundred; he had been a strict disciplinarian, but one much respected and, indeed, loved by his workforce who referred to him affectionately as 'The Governor'; he had handed on the torch to his sons, Ronald and Peter, but had been denied that privilege with his youngest son, Stephen who, in 1944 at the age of 21, had been killed on active service with the R.A.F. Ronald died suddenly in 1970 and Peter, as chairman, now heads the present board of directors. He has told of the past, and for the future assured me that his aim remains unaltered. 'Father's friendly courtesy to customers and staff alike will be retained. He always said "Honesty is the best policy. Do unto others as you would be done by," and I will keep faith with those words.'

Arcades are an integral part of the Leeds shopping habit. It has pedestrian precincts but the local housewife without her labyrinth of arcades—Thornton's, Queen's, County, to name but three of them—in which to shop and shop-window gaze would feel as bewildered as a Blackpool landlady without her Tower. No small wonder Snowden Schofield jumped at a shop in an arcade. Leave his arcade, pass through Thornton's Arcade, cross Briggate with the 'pelican' bleeper in our ear, to County Arcade and then turn up Vicar Lane to take a north-easterly direction to Hudson Road and another trader with a household name—**Montague Burton**.

Hudson Road Mills are easy to find. They are too large to miss. But to discover the personal story of Montague Burton who conceived this gigantic concourse is a more difficult task. Encomiums were anathema to him. He echoed Emerson's phrase, 'I like the silent church service before the service begins better than any preaching.' He was a doer not a talker; he was never fond of being interviewed, preferring to be known by work rather than by words; he has only the briefest of entries in *Who's Who*?—little beyond that he lived at Harrogate, married in 1909 and had three sons and a daughter. Difficult to build up a background story worthy of an enigmatic man who reigned supreme on one of Britain's clothing pinnacles? Let the Hudson Road factory tell its own story— the 'flesh on the bones' emerges quietly and unobtrusively.

The Hudson Road site covers a hundred acres and at one time found work for 20,000 employees. Montague Burton's first major factory was at Elmwood Mills but in 1914 he had taken larger premises with his Concord Street Mills and then in 1921, when he was about to acquire the title (and slogan) of 'the world's largest tailor' and the cry was for a still larger mill, this Harehills estate came onto the market. A hundred acres of rhubarb fields, interwoven with a fireclay works, a poultry farm and smallholding allotments. A typical West Riding conglomerated wilderness quickly transformed into a colossus of industry. The topic of Leeds conversation—the locals' wonder and pride. It was not unexpected that royalty would honour it in some future civic visit....it was inevitable. On 27th May 1931, Prince George was greeted there by the Lord Mayor, Dr. Arthur Hawkyard, and Montague.

By 1934 Montague felt his staff needed better facilities for taking their refreshments. He built a canteen where 8,000 could take a meal at one sitting and the Princess Royal came over from Harewood House to open it. He had always had a high place in his priorities for staff welfare and arranged that the ubiquitous 'cuppa' should be taken round to the benches, mornings and afternoons, at a penny a pot. But pots of tea were not the only things he dispensed in Hudson Road. There were facilities for dentistry, chiropody, optical treatment and for those away sick, extra financial benefits. Allied to these were pensions to which they could look forward, when pension schemes were a rarity rather than a right, bonuses, a works council with representatives from the shop floor, a staff magazine, various entertainment societies. Fifty years later these are taken for granted. When the Princess Royal came to Harehills they were 'perks' commanding the envy of many Leeds workforces. The tailors and tailoresses had come a long way from the turn of the century when a parliamentary committee had designated the Leeds clothing industry as second only to the sweat shops of London's East End, with work being carried out for long hours each day under deplorable conditions and at wages ranging from 26s to 50s a week for men and from 5s to 10s a week for women. When Montague Burton celebrated in 1950 his golden jubilee as a clothier and had built a £15,000,000 business, a well-known Member of Parliament came to Leeds to deliver a lecture on his pet theme and said of his visit, 'I went to Leeds with my head full of Walter Scott and I came back with it full of Montague Burton. Sir Walter Scott wrote romance. Sir Montague Burton lived one!'

Montague Burton was honoured with a knighthood in 1931, but remained always the same modest unassuming man. He found satisfaction in his knighthood being sponsored by a political party of which he was not a member.

His inbuilt business ability first showed signs of promise at the age of fifteen; he was shrewd enough at that early age to realise that the majority of men had much the same measurements and consequently can be fitted out for ready-made clothes. He borrowed £100 from a relative who not only trusted him but also showed confidence in the lad's new ideas. With this minute capital Montague opened in a modest way with a small scale clothing works. He knew his was the right idea and within ten years he had established a chain of High Street shops with 50-shilling suits in the not overcrowded windows. How attractive and irresistible they looked when worn by two or three good-looking 'dummies' standing on a parquet floor covering against a background of light brown grained decor. His suits were tasteful; his window-dressing was tasteful; and the courtesy of his assistants did the rest. Little wonder that the Concord Street mills were necessary and they in turn were replaced by the gigantic Hudson Road project.

By the time of his death in 1952, his horizons had extended far outside his commercial interests. Leeds benefitted by his munificence when in 1935 he helped in making possible the new University buildings. He also established chairs of Industrial and International Relations at several universities to study methods of ending industrial unrest and international conflict. His was a global outlook on life and he believed that modern civilisation would have to accept a system of world federation or perish. His suggestion was that Britain, the Commonwealth and the United States of America should take the first step in such a direction, with common laws, language, currency and a united police force. Perhaps he would have regarded the European Economic Community as a timorous beginning leading ultimately to something akin to his ideal. In addition to his knighthood, he did confide to his closest associates that the personal recognition which he most valued was membership of the writers' elite circle, the P.E.N. Club; his honorary Doctor of Laws conferred by Leeds University; and, rather a unique distinction, being offered the Lord Mayoralty although not a member of the city council. His own words perhaps summarise his life-commercial, 'It has ever been my aim to enable woolgrowers, wool processors, cloth makers and garment makers to enjoy good earnings and at the same time to reduce the margin between the price paid to the primary producer and the price charged to the customer.'

From Hudson Road we return to the city centre. We shall not lose our way for our bus has on its indicator board 'Via Corn Exchange' and that is our destination. Broderick's dignified, circular Corn Exchange, vastly under-rated architecturally, is now a central terminal for some of the corporation buses but it is also where thousands of 'loiners' have begun a holiday with a difference. At the Corn Exchange they have boarded a coach, left their worries behind, and headed for Scotland, the South Coast or perhaps the Continent. You name the place and it is more than likely that **Wallace Arnold** can take you there on one of their well-known tours.

The 'Wallace Arnold' saga is somewhat akin to that of the Thwaite Gate story. We went there expecting to hear of John Waddington and came away with the doings of Victor Watson. At the Corn Exchange it was reasonable to assume we should learn of Wallace Arnold's success in life; instead it was a fascinating tale of **Robert Barr**.

'Wallace Arnold' is a composite name based on two founders of a coach touring company which Robert Barr acquired on the eve of the 1926 General Strike. Wallace Cunningham was a late nineteenth century Leeds businessman well-known in local entertainment circles for his ventriloquilism. He teamed up with a younger man, Arnold Crowe, who died a blind octogenarian not many years ago in Morecambe. Between them they built up Wallace Arnold into a thriving coaching firm—small but with a reputation for personal every penny. The foreman, Arthur Claxton, who handed him his precious wage packet little thought that one day he would be this young man's chief engineer! He worked as much overtime as he could and to supplement his earnings he repaired cycles in the cellar of his digs. Gradually he saved sufficient to crystallise his dream of helping others to enjoy the Yorkshire countryside.

He bought his first motor-coach in 1912. He was proprietor, mechanic, driver and courier; a cog, albeit a small one, in the wheel of the tourist industry. His strict upbringing had inculcated into him the necessity of hard work, and those early lessons now stood him in good stead. Life had never been easy but now that he was his own master he found like all successful entrepreneurs that he had to work harder than ever. As for the motor-coach, that too was doing overtime. It was a goods vehicle from Monday morning until Friday night, when he changed the body, and Maskelyne-like, it emerged on Saturday morning as a symbol of pre-1914 freedom. It was a char-a-banc ready for its weekly jaunt to the dales or the coast.

This first experiment was stopped in its tracks by the outbreak of World War I, but in 1919 he re-sorted the bits and pieces, plunged with new energy into his interrupted career and the trips to the Yorkshire Dales were 'on' again. Soon he found that he needed other hands to help him. Arthur Claxton, his foreman from apprentice days, joined him to drive and repair the vehicles, an association which was to last many years. In 1921 he was taking West Riding citizens to Scotland, Devon and the South coast for a week's all-inclusive holiday—a marvellous innovation in those days. For Robert Barr a winning brainwave. That was the year in which he bought of Chas. H. Roe Ltd., Motor Body Builders of Crossgates, 'a new 30 seater char-a-banc body as quoted for £462. 10s.'

1924 and Robert confided to Arthur that he had plans for their biggest char-a-banc run yet.... a 400 mile round trip to Wembley and the great Empire Exhibition! At the time it seemed a daring venture, but its success was a major factor in his expansion. By the end of 1925 Robert Barr owned twenty-five vehicles and then came the purchase of the partnership of Wallace Cunningham and Arnold Crowe, for a price reputed to be less than £1,000, with Cunningham staying with the firm until his death in the 1940s. The other section of the business, which concerned itself with road haulage, bore the title R. Barr (Leeds) Ltd., and Robert's smart blue, gold and red waggons were known on trunk routes throughout the country.

In 1939 war again slowed down, but did not halt, the company's progress—or perhaps it would be more accurate to say that his lorries and coaches themselves went to war. His fleet covered on war service twenty *million* miles! For six years, a mileage equivalent to a journey around the world every alternate day. His lorries and coaches were in France in the phoney war days; on airfield construction work in service. Indeed, Arnold's wife, who lived to be over ninety, told me of her acting as courier on the early tours and was particularly fond of reminiscing on Edinburgh. It was these pioneers that Barr welded to his own branch of early motoring activities; he retained a name and built an outstanding success beyond the wildest dreams of either Wallace or Arnold—The Barr and Wallace Arnold Trust Ltd.

But we must go back to the turn of the century for the real beginnings......Robert Barr, born in Edinburgh in 1890, the eldest son of a large Scottish farming family, was brought south at an early age when his father took over the farm in Woolley, midway between Wakefield and Barnsley. He was an ambitious boy who, with the restlessness of youth, sensed new things 'in the air' as the nineteenth century moved into the twentieth. Even whilst driving the horses pulling the reaper in the harvest field, he would ponder on the arduous task of the men following behind, hand-tieing each sheaf of corn.

Mechanisation was at an embryonic stage on a farm but sufficient to set young Robert musing, 'Couldn't a machine be invented that would automatically tie up those sheaves as they were cut?' Dreams of youth swept aside as new-fangled nonsense by his conservative father. But the idea, and others, lingered on in his subconscious. He went to Wakefield market, to Barnsley cattle market, and was disturbed by the congestion and lack of loveliness in town life. The countryside meant so much to him and the fact that those people of the Yorkshire mining districts should not have easy and frequent access to it stuck in his mind. He was again, as he said later in life, 'dreaming the long, long dreams of youth'. But this time, he reacted more positively against his father's ridicule. If he could learn this new trade of motor-engineering, he felt he would be able to fulfil those vague thoughts that would keep constantly recurring. On a Saturday afternoon in December 1903 he slipped away to Leeds and persuaded the proprietor of the Bridge Garage to take him on as an apprentice, if his father would agree. Eventually dad was overcome, and although mother was much upset, both saw him off in January 1904 to lodgings in Beeston Hill, where he was to spend almost ten years working towards his goal—taking people to the countryside and giving them what he had always felt was their rightful heritage.

He often spoke of the hardships and difficulties of those apprenticeship days. A lad brought up on a farm is apt to feel overwhelmed by life in a big city; it is not easy to make friends amongst those with different backgrounds and tastes. He probably found an hour or two's relaxation in the Beeston 'lung', Cross Flatts Park, or walking across the 'poppy fields' to Far Beeston or the west woods of Middleton. When he could afford it he walked on the moors which were only a good bike ride from Leeds. But on a wage of five shillings a week, that only rose by two shillings a week each year until he was twenty-one, he would have to watch with care how to spend

Britain; on ack-ack sites and Home Guard duties; meeting the Dunkirk embarkation points; transporting prisoners of war to agricultural jobs. There seemed to be no end to the call and Robert himself not only supervised this fleet work but was also to take up an important post dealing with the establishment of government warehouses and the distribution of meat throughout Yorkshire, Northumberland and Durham. With these arduous and time-consuming duties he still found time to be Chief of the Auxiliary Fire Service in Leeds!

Coming home late one night in March 1944, he received the news that his eldest son, also named Robert, had been killed on active service with the Fleet Air Arm. Snowden Schofield and Robert Barr had to shoulder the same onerous cross within a few days of each other. To lose a child in early manhood is one of the most bitter-tasting cups in life; it must have been a grievous burden added to an already heavy load.

The war was at last behind and there came a dramatic demand for relaxation—and that for many meant holiday travel. With his usual foresight Robert Barr had purchased in 1942 an old-established coachbuilding firm and this paid an immense dividend in putting his coaching fleet back on the road when other operators found it well nigh impossible to renew their vehicles. In 1946 he was offering an inclusive week in Bournemouth for £15.

1958 was a great year for his motoring 'empire', for it saw the completion of a new depot in Hunslet Road opened by Lord Brabazon of Tara. But it was almost the end of the road for Robert Barr, Leeds' adopted son who had been content to accept five shillings a week to be taught the craft of motor repairing and had seen his company grow from one char-a-banc to a great and diverse concern giving employment to many and pleasure to thousands more. He died in 1961 and those who knew him best summed up his life:- 'Robert Barr in spite of his "empire" was no remote emperor. The interest he had shown as a boy in his fellow human beings had never left him and his death was mourned by many from all walks, not least by those who had worked for him.'

During his fire-watching days he had prepared notes for a book, *I Travel the Road*, published in 1945, which expounded his philosophy and his aims. He quotes Lord Bacon, 'Travel in the younger sort is part of education; in the elder, a part of experience.' Those words seem to give the clue in his life's work.

We are under the clock at Dyson's again, ready to move on to other parts of the city to meet more of Leeds' personalities. Some words of Wordsworth, written of a cogent Lakeland character, will persist in my mind. Words which exactly describe each of the great traders whom we have visited: 'Brief notices of his life ought to find a place in the Histories.'

3. Courage and Adventure

Fl. Sgt. Aaron V.C.—Geoffrey Appleyard—Dave Clarke

THERE is a fount of material to prove that Leeds citizens have without hesitation accepted the challenge when duty has set it before them. It is fitting that we relate first, one on whom was posthumously conferred the highest award and whose citations concluded with the words: 'An example of devotion to duty which has been seldomed equalled, never surpassed.' Official citations are not given to encomiastic cliches. They speak the truth. So 'let us now praise famous men'.

Arthur Louis Aaron's life span was short when measured in time—a mere twenty-one years—but in that brief period he achieved greatness. He was born in 1922 and resided at 40, Hartley Grove. Even in pre-school days he had shown stickability. 'England's highest mountain, Scafell Pike with its 3,210ft peak, is not an easy jaunt, whether you slog from Wasdale Head or Rosset Ghyll. To sit astride the summit cairn at the age of five indicates an individuality and a personality that will attain life's heights. Only sixteen years separate Arthur Aaron's conquest of Scafell and his conquest of the skies over Italy. His father, after his son's death, emphasised this tenacity of purpose, 'He was extremely quiet and somewhat shy but the pertinacity which he displayed in his achievement had always been conspicuous in his character.'

Aaron was educated at Roundhay School and his is the first name on the roll in the *Roundhegian,* the supplement to the school magazine dealing with the Old Boys in the Services. His headmaster referred to him as a boy with plenty of spirit, like his brother Frank—later a physician and a noted northern cross-country runner, 'In school, Arthur controlled that spirit very well and conducted himself in a dignified way, but the spirit was there. He was an able boy, particularly in art, and he was a good athlete, though he did more running than cricket and other games. With his brother Frank he could be seen going out at night across the countryside and through

Roundhay Park. They were both excellent runners.'

Leaving school in 1939, he moved to the architectural section of the Leeds College of Art and remained into his second year. He was spoken of as a promising student of marked ability, popular with both staff and fellow-students alike. His family said he was mad on aeroplanes and it was no surprise that he served as a cadet in the Leeds University Air Squadron and joined the Volunteer Reserve of the Royal Air Force in 1941, qualifying for his 'wings' in Texas. By 1942 he was back in this country on operational flying. A foretaste of the future ultimate honour was seen in his being awarded the Distinguished Flying Medal. At the time of his death he had completed nineteen operational flights, many of them against strongly defended German targets and his logbook recorded ninety hours of operational flying. The D.F.M. was in recognition of several successful sorties, and in particular on the occasion when a fire had broken out in the rear of the bomb door. The wireless operator and flight engineer managed to control the outbreak and meanwhile Flt. Sgt. Aaron had pressed home his attack on the target, undistressed by the perilous situation of the aircraft. 'Pertinacity of purpose'—how right his father had described him.

1943. The year in which young Aaron was destined to become the only indigenous boy to be awarded the Victoria Cross during World War II. One can imagine the swelling pride of the boys of Roundhay School as their headmaster told them the news and its details. He read:-

The King has been graciously pleased to convey the VICTORIA CROSS on the undermentioned airman in recognition of most conspicuous bravery:-

1458181 Acting Flight Sergeant Arthur Louis AARON D.F.M., Royal Air Force Volunteer Reserve (deceased), No 218 Squadron.

On the night of 12th August, 1943, F/Sgt. Aaron was captain and pilot of a Stirling aircraft detailed to attack Turin. When approaching to attack, the bomber received devastating bursts of fire from an enemy fighter. Three engines were hit, the windscreen shattered, the front and rear turrets put out of action and the elevator control damaged, causing the aircraft to become unstable and difficult to control. The navigator was killed and other members of the crew were wounded.

A bullet struck F/Sgt. Aaron in the face, breaking his jaw and tearing away part of his face. He was also wounded in the lung and his right arm was rendered useless. As he fell forward over the control column, the aircraft dived several thousand feet. Control was regained by the flight engineer at 3,000 feet. Unable to speak, F/Sgt. Aaron urged the bomb aimer by signs to take over the controls. Course was then set southwards in an endeavour to fly the crippled bomber, with one engine out of action, to Sicily or North Africa. F/Sgt. Aaron was assisted to the rear of the aircraft and treated with morphia. After resting for some time he rallied and, mindful of his responsibility of the aircraft, insisted on returning to the pilot's cockpit, where he was lifted into his seat and had his feet placed on the rudder bar. Twice he made determined attempts to take control and hold the aircraft on its course, but his weakness was evident, and with difficulty he was persuaded to desist. Though in great pain and suffering exhaustion, he continued to help by writing directions with his left hand.

Five hours after leaving the target the petrol began to run low, but soon afterwards the flare path at Bone airfield was sighted. F/Sgt. Aaron summoned his failing strength to direct the bomb aimer in the hazardous task of landing the damaged aircraft in the darkness with the undercarriage retracted. Four attempts were made under his direction; at the fifth F/Sgt. Aaron was so near collapsing that he had to be restrained by the crew and the landing was completed by the bomb aimer.

Nine hours after landing, F/Sgt. Aaron died from exhaustion. Had he been content, when grievously wounded, to lie still and conserve his failing strength, he would probably have recovered, but he saw it as his duty to exert himself to the utmost, if necessary with his last breath, to ensure that his aircraft and crew did not fall into enemy hands. In appalling conditions he showed the greatest qualities of courage, determination and leadership, and though wounded and dying he set an example of devotion to duty which has seldom been equalled and never surpassed.

Thus reads Royal Air Force Award No. 695. Little wonder that the citizens of Leeds, deeply moved at his great ability, hastened in their only tangible way of expressing their esteem of such a worthy son of the city. They unstintingly supported a memorial fund to create a scholarship at the School of Architecture for boys from Roundhay and other Leeds secondary schools.

How proud Aaron's parents, when H.M. King George VI handed to them their son's medal with the words: 'It was a very brave act that your son did, in bringing his aeroplane and crew to safety.'

Little did I know, serving with the First Army, as I passed Bone Airfield in those August days of 1943 that a fellow 'loiner' had been laid to rest nearby. He lies there, in Annaba (the new Algerian name for Bone) War cemetery, his one of a thousand graves so immaculate, so well tended and lovingly cared for—as are all the North African war cemeteries that I have visited in recent years. The uniform headstones, each with the R.A.F. or regimental badge, each with a message engraved at the foot as requested by their nearest and dearest, stand like troops on a reveille parade—but their call has come on the other side. The simple inscription on his stone, '1458181 Fl. Sgt. A.L. Aaron V.C., D.F.M., Pilot R.A.F. 14.8.1943, age 21. An example of courage seldom equalled but never surpassed' was, by a coincidence, engraved by a Leeds man, Jack Fielding, working as a mason with the Royal Engineers.

It is beyond understanding that there was a person in Leeds who in 1946 could burgle the Aaron home and steal the irreplaceable medals and other family treasures. However, following a national appeal, even the culprit had a sufficient spark of common decency to repent and return the Victoria Cross and the D.F.M. medal, whilst retaining the remainder of the booty. Since 1953 the awards have been in the safekeeping of the Leeds City Museum.

We remember Arthur Louis Aaron and the words he made his own 'Courage seldom equalled, never surpassed.' What an ideal for the present generation of Roundhay boys to keep before them.

In addition to Fl. Sgt. Aaron, Leeds is proud to have had 16 other V.C.'s, ten of them natives of the city and the others with residential associations.

We have seen how two leading traders knew the heartbreak of sons lost on active service. The founder of a third firm, the motor factors, Appleyard of Leeds, also lost a son serving overseas. J.E. Appleyard wrote the courageous exploits of his son, **Geoffrey Appleyard**, and it was published under the simple arresting title of *Geoffrey*. I wonder if Robert Barr wrote his tale of the road as a similar solace for deep felt grief. There seems a coincidental link in two fathers turning to the pen.

Major John Geoffrey Appleyard, D.S.O., M.C. and Bar, M.A. (Cantab.); popularly known as 'Apple'; Commando and Special Air Service Regiment; a 'loiner' from Bramley, born on 20th December 1916, whose full and self-sacrificial life the city recalls with justifiable pride. His family moved from Bramley to Linton-on-Wharfe near Wetherby in 1921 and after attending the local village school, Geoffrey went to Moorlands School at Headingley, and then, when he was fifteen, Bootham School, York. One of his outstanding traits was emphasised by his housemaster, who, in his report, wrote: 'I admire his absolute straightforwardness; it seems to be the pattern on which he builds his life.' Looking at his photograph I was immediately struck that his frankness shows through. 1935 found him at Caius College, Cambridge, where water-skiing rather than rowing attracted him, but it was as a skier on the snow of the Swiss Alps that he eventually won a 'blue'. He took a 'first' in B.A. engineering and joining his father in 1938 seemed set for a career in the motoring world. But the year of fate, 1939, intervened, and, on the Supplementary Reserve of Officers, he was mobilised with the R.A.S.C. at the outbreak of war. 1940 was for him an eventful year. He escaped on the overthrow of France through Dunkirk and that year he met re-armament of a different order, Moral Re-Armament. For the remainder of his short span of life he was a keen follower of Frank Buchman and his M.R.A. Group—the old Oxford Group as it was originally termed in this country.

On his return to England, all ranks of the Army were informed of the formation of nuclei of specially trained men to be known as 'commandos'. They were to be an elite body with the ability to act as small raiding parties to sting the Nazis whenever and wherever it was feasible. It made an instant appeal to young Appleyard—who volunteered and moved to the West coast of Scotland for secret training. Realizing the hazards which most certainly would lay ahead, he wrote to his family, 'don't pray for my safety or for my speedy return but pray that I am alive to my responsibilities, courageous in danger and that I have the strength to do my bit of a job to the utmost. Remember I am responsible for 25 men—I mustn't let them down. Pray, too, that I am continually sensitive to the real "Commander-in-chief" for then I can have continual guidance and my "lines of communication" can never be cut!'

The spring of 1941 saw him aboard a submarine bound for the Bay of Biscay and detailed to bring back two French secret service agents. He completed this mission but only by displaying tenacity of purpose of the highest order. German patrols were encountered, the Frenchmen were unable to display the agreed signals, and 'Apple's' ration of time before the submarine was to depart with or without the raiding party had almost expired, but he waited and made contact with his allies. They were rescued, he took them to the sub in an inflated rubber dinghy and he received the first of his honours — the Military Cross. The same spring he qualified at Ringway, Manchester, for his parachute wings and was asked to join as second-in-command Captain Gus March-Phillips. With him he was to select from their commandos and from other sources a small group who, as a tightly woven unit, would train, not only for amphibious duties but to work out their own schemes for raiding the enemy. They asked for a Brixham trawler *Maid Honor*, and, berthed at Poole Harbour they worked steadily towards their first plan — the raiding of a large enemy liner and two smaller craft which were thought to be anchored in a distant port. This initial skirmish was successfully accomplished and the three enemy ships were captured and sailed home.

In August, Appleyard and the *Maid Honor* were in the Freetown-Lagos area of West Africa on a most important mission — to ascertain where and to what extent the enemy submarines were re-fuelling in that part of the world. What they were seeking was a key to the Battle of the Atlantic. 'Apple found out much information and returned to the United Kingdom to learn he had to collect a Bar to his Military Cross — his reward for capturing the liner and its acolytes.

Lord Mountbatten, Chief of Combined Operations, was beginning to take notice of Appleyard and his colleagues. Gus and Geoffrey were instructed by him to set up a south coast base — again they chose Poole — to train men (mainly commando officers) in the use of motor launches and to prepare plans for a Small Scale Raiding Force against the French coast. This proved to be one of his toughest training periods ever — long jumping not 'a l'Olympic' fashion but over extensive pits packed with barbed wire, not the most comfortable of landing nets; crossing rivers on a rope bridge made up on the spot with toggle ropes carried by each man....and in the river beneath *live* mines were anchored; scaling apparently unclimbable cliffs with more ropes; sailing exercises in the Channel when it was deemed un-safe for the normal use of boats. All those who later thought they were being sadistically treated at O.C.T.U. en route to *their* commissions blessed the unknown creators of some of these frolicsome games. How Geoff Appleyard's ears must have burned!

These men tested their ideas in capturing Cassquets lighthouse and put its machinery out of action. Appleyard broke his ankle on this trip but three nights later he was with the raiding party again, directing, instead of leading, from the launch. He submitted an idea for a two-man submarine, but at that time it did not meet with official approval.

'Apple' was well aware he was liable to dice with death and his friend Gus summed up their feelings thus:-

Let me be brave and gay again,
O Lord, when my time is near,
Let the good in me rise up and break
The stranglehold of fear;
Say that I die for Thee and the King,
And what I hold most dear.

Lines written immediately prior to a fateful raid on 12th September 1942, when March-Phillips was killed, others captured and Appleyard brought the much depleted party back to port. This was the fore-runner of an even more daring assault on one of the Channel Islands—a raid in which five officers of the group of ten collected a Victoria Cross, a D.S.O. and three M.C.s between them. He was summoned to Winston Churchill's room to receive congratulations, the C.I.G.S also sent for him and in December he found himself again at Buckingham Palace to collect the D.S.O. award for his part in many cross-Channel raids. The King, always reputed to have the right phrase at the right time, greeted him, 'What, you here again so soon.'

All in all he took part in no less than seventeen of these raids in which landings were made on the enemy coast, whilst there were innumerable reconnaissances close in shore from which he returned with his sought-for information without having had to land.

The First Army made its North Africa landings and Appleyard's No. 1 Small Scale Raiding Force had 'B.N.A.F.' added to its address. They were now working from Oran, Algiers and any convenient base which furthered their plans. He flew to Malta to carry out reconnaissance work for submarines and became a legendary figure within the First Army. General Alexander requested that he survey Pantelleria, the small island which was a stepping stone to Sicily and Italy and had a garrison strongly fortified by 13,000 troops. That he was successful is a matter of history—Pantelleria was subsequently captured and the way cleared for the follow-up to the Italian mainland. Leeds certainly played an important role in the invasion and re-conquest of Europe.

June 1943 and the Army felt that, although he himself had never given it a thought, a six months' rest from operational duties would safeguard his vitality and nervous system for future work. Looking back on the saga of courage and leadership it is not surprising that such a rest was deemed to be imperative. The ironical part of the decision is that it was the step which led to his early death.

His last letter home, dated 6th July 1943, tells of his going away from his camp for two or three weeks but that he should receive his mail at intervals. Those words foretold of his last task. He was to embark on a tour to arrange for an airborne expedition in which some of his commandos were to be dropped in Sicily, capture and hold a strategic bridge and ease the way for the Allied landings. His brother officers said that *he* must not make the drop into Sicily. He went to Kairouan to supervise his commandos' flight. On the night of 12th July he telephoned headquarters asking permission for a recce flight that night as the conditions were perfect. Later a despatch rider arrived at H.Q. stating that he had decided to go on the flight himself in order to be sure of the best landing place for his men and with a view to determining the spot to which follow-up reinforcements should be sent. He stated that he expected to be back about 1 a.m. It is assumed that he did not mention his intentions when speaking earlier on the telephone for fear of permission to fly being refused. He did not return and he was probably shot down on the return journey. His flight was so typical of 'Apple'. He wanted to be sure he had done his best for his men.

Leslie Weatherhead, the world-famous minister of Brunswick, Leeds from 1925 to 1936, once commented; 'I knew Geoffrey from his schooldays onwards. At the time of his early manhood I said to a friend, "If a visitor dropped down from Mars and visited each country to find out what the Earth's inhabitants were like and if I had a chance to suggest whom such a visitor should meet in England I should suggest Geoffrey Appleyard." His love of adventure, his sense of humour, his self-forgetfulness, his chivalry, his love of birds and poetry and his unobtrusive but real religion were all woven into the texture of a character as strong and beautiful as any I have ever known. Perhaps all can be summed up by saying that he revelled in life—physically, mentally and spiritually—and made all with whom he came into contact feel that life was a good thing as he lived it. Nothing could persuade me that this gay troubadour is dead. His body he may have given for England but his soul lives on—part of the wealth of the universe for it possessed qualities that do not die and over which war has no power'.

From wartime exploits to an expedition no less arduous, no less exciting—the ascent of Mount Everest. Since man decided that he *would* stand on the topmost peak of the topmost mountain, the conquest of Everest has been irresistible to mountaineers. Having looked at Everest at close quarters from the comfort of a small Nepalese 'plane I can vividly picture what that challenge must have implied.

Coronation year 1953 saw Hillary and Sherpa Tensing astride that Himalayan summit—but man was still not satisfied. After Hillary's success, his traverse would be looked upon as the *conventional* path. Man must needs find a more difficult route. Chris Bonington did—as he describes in his book *Everest—The Hard Way*. In the Bonington team, as we might have expected from our growing knowledge of Leodensians, the city had its man—**Dave Clarke.**

LEADERS OF INDUSTRY

Above: Joshua Tetley, founder of a great Yorkshire brewery.

Left: Sir Ernest Woodroofe, born at Leeds in 1912, rose to become chairman of Unilever—the tenth largest company in the world.

Victor H. Watson, who by means of such games as 'Lexicon' and 'Monopoly' made the firm of John Waddington Ltd a household name.

Snowden Schofield (right), who came to Leeds with £300 in his pocket and opened a small two-windowed shop in Victoria Arcade (opposite, top). From this modest beginning has sprung today's vast store (above).

Cockburn High School, off Dewsbury Road, 'a red-brick, no-nonsense centre of learning' where several now-famous Leeds 'loiners' received their education—Sir Ernest Woodroofe, Willis Hall, Richard Hoggart and Stella Shock (now Mrs Frankie Vaughan).

A Wallace Arnold coach tour to Paignton in 1928. This then small coaching firm had been bought two years earlier for a price reputed to be under £1,000 by Robert Barr, who built it up into the present-day 'holiday empire'.

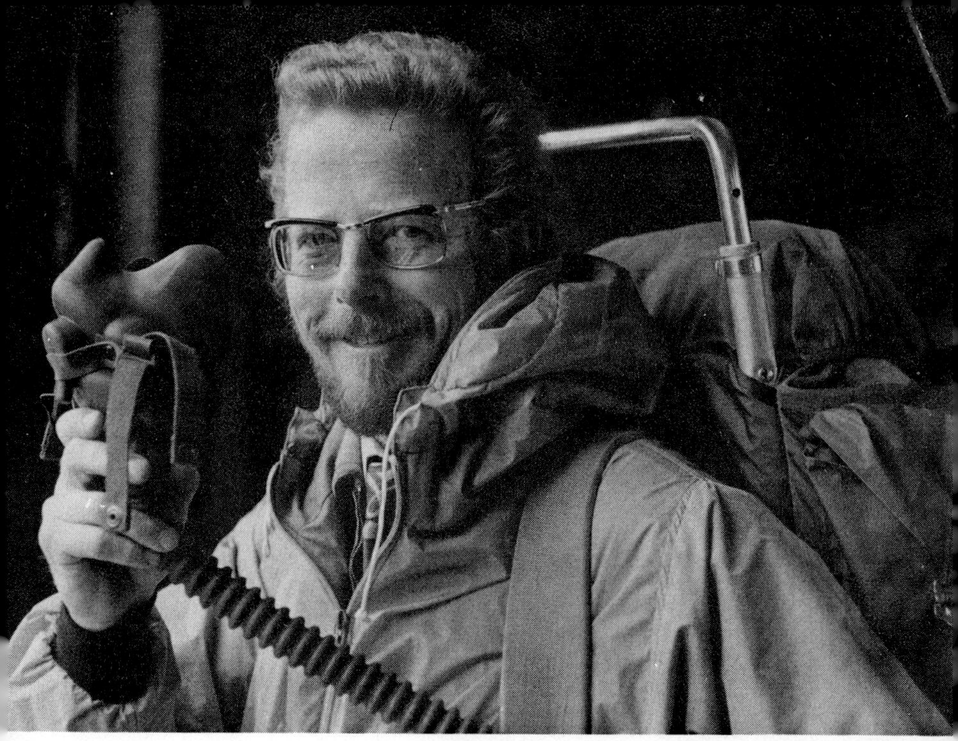

Above: Dave Clarke, Himalayan climber and equipment organiser for Chris Bonington's 1975 Everest expedition.

Right: Arthur Louis Aaron, posthumously awarded the Victoria Cross in 1942 in recognition of exceptional bravery. (Yorkshire Post Newspapers Ltd)

THE WORLD OF THE ARTS

Above: Michael Roll, winner of the Leeds International Pianoforte Competition in 1963.

Left: Sir William Linton Andrews, editor of the Leeds Mercury and then the Yorkshire Post, who played a leading part in starting the 1936 abdication crisis of Edward VIII. (Yorkshire Post Newspapers Ltd)

LEEDS-BORN WRITERS

Above: Keith Waterhouse (left) and Willis Hall, dramatists and writers whose productions have been seen in theatres on both sides of the Atlantic.

Left: Richard Hoggart, born at Chapeltown in 1918 and now enjoying a place of eminence in the world of literature and education. (Yorkshire Post Newspapers Ltd)

SPORTING CELEBRITIES

Above: Geoff Gunney, who played for Hunslet for no less than 23 years from 1951 to 1974.

Left: Eddie Waring, the indomitable Rugby League commentator. (Yorkshire Post Newspapers Ltd)

'South West Face—British Everest Expedition 1975, sponsored by Barclays Bank International' was the official title of the new climb and it was in that body of mountaineers that Clarke found himself Equipment Organiser. Bonington wanted someone in the equipment business who would have the expertise for tackling the mammoth task which would confront him. He remembered that Clarke, who ran a climbing shop in Leeds, had in 1972 volunteered to go with him as an unpaid Sherpa, and how previously Dave had been with him on an expedition to South Patagonia carrying out a geological survey. It was following this that Clarke found himself helping to build a bridge at Backbarrow near the southern end of Windermere and in 1967 taking a job as a quarry manager in Coniston. During these spells in the Lake District he had again met Chris and climbed on several occasions with him. In 1968 both had been involved in an attempt to canoe down the upper reaches of the River Inn in Switzerland. It seemed to Bonington that Dave was his man. He later said of him, 'He was a hard worker, a perfectionist in everything he did and yet, at the same time, had a warm sense of humour and a real consideration for the people with whom he was working......he fully justified the confidence I put in him, the ideal person for this formidable task.'

The job of organising the equipment was most complex. Not only had a group of eighteen climbers to be kitted out but also a BBC film team of four, a *Sunday Times* journalist, thirty-eight high-altitude Sherpas, thirty other porters and a large number of base personnel. Dave packed a Leeds warehouse with a myriad of items of gear. How it was to fit into two lorries was impossible to see but that was only part of his problems. The instructions from Bonington were to keep an accurate record of the contents of each box he packed. He had to know which were to be off-loaded at Kathmandu, which to be sent through to Khumde near the foot of Everest and which to go straight through to Base Camp. As he also explained each load had to be weatherproofed and had not to exceed the maximum carry of sixty pounds for the Sherpas. He worked for eighteen hours a day, helped by a group of Boy Scouts, and spent two days loading two lorries. The labours of Clarke were on their way to Everest—a journey of 7,000 miles and 24 days in front of them.

July 1975, and he was in the team flying to Kathmandu; August, and he was taking his place on the long approach march to Khumde and on to the Base Camp on the lower slopes of the mountain. There he was occupied juggling with the issue of personal equipment to over a hundred men, Europeans and Asians, but, in Bonington's own words, 'he went from strength to strength and did a superb job of organising'. On 9th September he took his allotted climbing place in the team at Camp 2 at a level of 21,600 feet. He was playing a full part in a tremendous feat and his arrival at this altitude meant that the 'lead climbers' could move nearer their objective. He was in charge of Camp 2 with the day to day running of it, together with detailed movement of the porters. In this game of mountaineering 'leap-frog' he did not remain at the lower camp; 21st September saw him at 23,700 feet running Camp 4, and again freeing men for the assault on the summit. In the event of failure by the first group he would have accompanied Bonington, with two others, to make a final bid to crown the expedition with the success they so keenly sought. 'Equipment organiser' certainly covered a multitude of activities but here was proof of the high esteem in which he was held as a Himalayan climber. In the event he was not called upon for this ultimate effort for four of his comrades attained the summit.

The retreat from the mountain was fraught with as much danger as the climb; one colleague, Burke, had been lost surging as a 'lead climber' for the top peak; the ice-fields were beginning to slide and Clarke was involved in the race against time. But on the last day of September, all were clear of the icefall and thirty-three days in his life, days full of courage and comradeship, determination and danger, were forever etched in his mountain memories. The 38 year old family man had not left his wife and two children and his shop in Woodhouse Lane in vain. He had succeeded. He had given his unstinted best—a willing member of a closely-knit group. To be 'one of Bonington's men' was a title of which to be proud—a heritage to hand down to his youngsters.

In Dave Clarke's words his greatest pleasure on the expedition was the time spent at Camp 4. There 'I was an active part of the climbing effort in a fantastic camp and free of the equipment organiser's title. In that unglamorous role one is inevitably pre-occupied with impersonal lists of equipment and loading schedules, with little time to relax and enjoy people rather than packing. One eventually resents the situation but it seems to go with the job and one has to look for satisfaction to the successful maintenance of equipment flowing up and down the mountain and feel that it does all help to put the team on top.'

And the worrying moments of the '75 expedition?

'The worry started in the year preceding when making preparations for the equipment but the high spot occurred during the drive out to Nepal and the report came back of bandits attacking the two trucks. There was always an element of fear until 'on the spot' distribution of every part of the stores proved I hadn't forgotten anything. But on the climb itself I think the fear came to the front again when I heard of the two deaths which occurred in the party. In addition to Mick Burke we had also earlier lost a young Sherpa whom I had got to know very well. 'Most satisfaction, apart from actual pleasure? Well, I was a retailer buying priceless gear and to get it at a third of the price was good. Then, resisting the panic when Bonington felt that "we'd taken on more than he had done before and wasn't sure we could do it". And, too, it was most gratifying, as equipment man, to be able to satisfy the almost impossible high standards of the "lead" climbers who were understandably critical of life protecting equipment.'

I wonder how you felt when you stood at Camp 4 with the world of ice and snow encompassing you around? 'Simple! First time jiggered; second time satisfied; third time—and during the occupancy—elated! 'You ask if there are any other parts of the world other than the Himalayas which especially appeal. First of all, I think I should confess that, as well as tennis, squash and badminton I have developed an absorbing interest in ski-ing. I would love to go to North America and Canada and to sample helicopter ski-ing would be fantastic. My memories of Patagonia are unforgettable. Yes, I would like to visit there again. I remember, too, several journeys of two or three months duration in Swedish Lappland and others in the European Alps. But no matter what part of the world attracts, my first love of the Lake District cannot be usurped as my "mountain home". Of all the spots, whilst it is impossible to dogmatise, I think I would choose Eagle Crag, Birkness Combe, with Buttermere behind me and Pillar in front—marvellous.'

Have you any other hobbies?

'Only one - people. People are my hobby at all times. People interest me - always.'

I asked Dave if he would tell me of his background in the pre-Everest days. I could not have wished for a more willing co-operator.

'I'm not a "loiner", as you term it; I was born on 24th August 1937 at West Hartlepool, and came in 1947 to live at 21, Upper Carr Lane, Calverley. I went to school there and followed with a spell at Salt High School, Shipley. From there I embarked on civil engineering studies at Leeds University. Meanwhile, all my friends seemed to be connected with the Methodist chapel in Calverley and I joined them—and the Scouts. I must confess though I eventually became what I suppose could be called a lapsed Methodist.'

Then we turned to how his love of climbing first began. He chuckled, 'It was a friend at Salt High School who started it all. When cross-country time came round we sneaked off to Shipley Glen and sampled rock-climbing. So really the Glen was the first of the steps to the upper slopes of Everest!'

Did you marry a local girl?'

'No, a Lancashire lass whom I met in the climbing club at the University. 1959 to 1966 saw me busy as a civil engineer on the hydro-electric scheme in Scotland and then a couple of years bridge-building on the M6 motorway preceded the spell in the Lakes. I was never far away from the mountains but I decided to set up a climbing equipment shop in Leeds in 1968 and this carried on through the Everest days, providing a base for other "adventuring" activities too, until 1980. I have enjoyed all my various professional enterprises, but as my two youngsters have now moved out to University, I am ready and able to tackle something new, when the "inspiration" strikes. My wife and I are still relatively young and this gives a great flexibility in deciding the next phase of our life. At the moment we haven't honestly decided on our next move.'

I liked the 'we' and the 'our life.' Words used by a dedicated family man. One felt what a wealth of adventure and courage had been packed into such a relatively short span. For the youth of today setting out for a life of satisfaction here was a philosopher guide ready to be tapped. His advice to them?

'Know yourself first and satisfaction can almost be guaranteed.'

And the secret of success?

'I am not being flippant when I reply "what success"? I am generally speaking, very happy with my position and achievements in life. If people see that as success then I assume that the position accords with their own idea of success. I have no real concept of "success". An assessment of my life at this point in time? I think a fair answer would be to say that, firstly, I have reached a stage where outward status and acclaim are not necessary, even undesirable, and that, secondly, I have identified the importance to me of challenge and therefore will ensure that this element is present in future activities in one way or another. Expeditions are an obvious "adventure" and whilst I am physically able will undertake all I can.'

Are there any other personal reflections you would like to make?

'Over the years I have always been moved by a curiosity and energy to try any new experience and I feel now that I will always do so. All my experience so far points to the value of this approach so I have:

'Parachuted and potholed, arranged flowers and played squash, tried my hand at sculpting and broadcasting to hospital patients. Read a lot and liked pop and classical music. Adventured on my own but raised a family successfully I think. The message is variety and for somebody I admired to assess me as a "well-balanced" man would be the ultimate compliment. My hope is that I always have been quite well balanced and the adding of years of experience doesn't alter the balance—merely the weight added as I go along to both sides of my character.'

And finally two questions of perhaps a lighter nature but drawing forth serious replies. Any pet dislikes? As a northerner, any trait which especially appeals?

'Pet dislikes—self-important people; northerners—their sense of humour and their acceptance of the work ethic, knowing it to be such a life destroying distribution, really.'

I bid him adieu remembering words of Blake:

Great things are done when men and mountains meet,
This is not done by jostling in the street.

4. The Arts

Fanny Waterman — Michael Roll — Henry Moore — Storm Jameson — Linton Andrews — Richard Hoggart

SE 298339. If one was given the task of geographically pinpointing the arts centre in Leeds there is the O.S. map reference which would lead to the Leeds Town Hall, the City Art Gallery, Museum and Central Library. The Town Hall, the setting of the Leeds Musical Festival and the triennial Leeds International pianoforte competition, has a great hall which Broderick could have designed with these musical extravaganza especially in mind. Under royal patronage—Yorkshire's own Duchess of Kent—the presidency of the Lord Mayor and a noble array of vice-presidents, lies the guiding hand of Miss Fanny Waterman O.B.E., M.A., F.R.C.M., assisted by Mrs Jeremy Thorpe.

Fanny Waterman is a daughter of Leeds and it is her story that we now hear. I am indebted to her for so readily giving me all the information for which I troubled her. She is a 'loiner', educated at Allerton High School and Leeds University, and now lives at Roundhay, is married to Dr. Geoffrey de Keyser and is the mother of two sons. She occupies a pre-eminent position in the piano-teaching world. She studied first with Tobias Matthay and later, after winning a scholarship to the London Royal College of Music, with Cyril Smith. Student prizes followed and, while still at college, she began making public appearances as a concert pianist. The acclaim that greeted her performances, particularly at the Promenade Concerts, seemed to point to a notable performing career. She felt, however, that teaching was her real vocation and she returned to Leeds, where she embarked on a career that has made her one of the most conspicuously successful piano teachers of our time. Even in 1969 *The Times* could refer to her as 'the now legendary Fanny Waterman'. In the succeeding years her ever-growing list of prize-winning pupils—Paul Crossley, Michael Roll, Allan Schiller, to name but a few—has brought her a renown that extends far beyond the confines of England.

Fanny Waterman's extraordinary success as a teacher stems from her concentration on security of technique placed at the disposal of imagination and musicianship. One of her secrets has been to convey to her pupils a sense of excitement by working through their imaginative abilities right from the start. 'Of course', she said, 'a sure technical grounding is essential and I am a firm believer in discipline and technique, but as a mutual discovery of human and musical qualities.

Her enthusiasm and industry is not, however, confined to her own private pupils. Her determination to raise the standards of piano playing generally, led her in 1963 to found jointly with Marion Harewood, now Mrs Jeremy Thorpe, the Leeds International Pianoforte Competition of which she is chairman. It was an immediate success and is established as one of the world's major competitions. The idea had been conceived more than two years before and they learned at the outset that being musicians is not sufficient in itself to promote and manage an international competition. They found the need for a practical knowledge of the workings and reactions of councils, committees and voluntary workers, several extra thicknesses of skin and, more important than anything, the ability to ignore the word 'NO'. All that is now past history. Two years of hard work and excitement, together with their fair share of frustration and disappointment, finally resulted in a competition whose artistic standards led to its immediate acclaim as being of regional, national, and international importance.

Fanny Waterman reiterated that they made many true friends over the years. 'Even if some of them are no longer with us, we shall never forget the part they played. Benjamin Britten presented the first competition with a piece he had specially composed for the occasion, "Notturno". It was a beautiful and evocative piece, and reminded us deeply of his life and the inspiration he gave to all musicians, young and old.'

She continued, 'When I sit behind the jury on the opening day of each competition I still find it hard to believe that such a distinguished group of musicians from all over the world should turn down lucrative engagements and freely give of their time to sit on hard benches listening to piano-playing for ten hours a day.'

More recently Fanny Waterman has been expanding her teaching activities to include radio and television and has lectured at the Royal Society of Arts, the Incorporated Society of Musicians and the International Society for Music Education. She has given Master Classes at many festivals and teaching centres throughout England and abroad, as far afield as Iceland, Australia and Japan. The acuteness of her ear, her illuminating turn of phrase, her comprehensive technical knowledge have helped all who have participated. She has also been much in demand as a jury member at international piano competitions and has officiated in Vienna, Terni, Leipzig and

Munich.

With such an imposing array of achievements to her name it is not surprising that in recognition of her services to music, Fanny Waterman has been awarded an O.B.E., an honorary M.A. from Leeds University and an F.R.C.M. For our first pen-picture from the local arts scene we could have no better representative than her and it would seem a natural step to her gifted pupil and now virtuoso in his own right, **Michael Roll**.

John Michael Frederick Roll is the son of a doctor practising in Moortown. He was born on 17th July 1946 at the Buckingham Nursing Home in Clarendon Road and his earliest years were spent in Easterly Road before his family moved to the 'West Parks' adjacent to Street Lane—at the age when sledging down the slightly hilly 'Kingswoods' was a winter attraction. That district has an excellent primary school set amidst attractive playing fields, Talbot Road School, and that is where young Michael Roll first heard about the three 'R's. He moved to Roundhay School and was working hard with the Medical School as his target—how these Leeds men love to follow their fathers—when chance played its hand. He won the 1963 Leeds pianoforte competition. Marlowe was right—'For will in us is overruled by fate'.

How proud Fanny Waterman, along with his parents, must have been on the September evening when an eminent jury agreed that Michael Roll's playing had outshone and withstood the intense competition of the international field. When I spoke to Michael recently I did not ask what his feelings were at that youthful moment of triumph. It was not an omission. His quiet voice and manner bespoke of an ingrained modesty which was so impressive that I felt it would be an intrusion to ask him to enlarge on what must have been, until then, *the* moment of his life. I remember one incident that was typical of this self-effacing modesty. He rang up one evening to clarify one or two points and I mentioned that it was a coincidence that he should telephone as I was listening to a B.B.C. recital of Greig's piano concerto. He immediately offered to hang up and ring again later so that I should not forego any of my listening. That simple but telling gesture remains in my memory as an incident of his genuine kindly concern for others. It was the mark of a great man.

When he triumphed at Leeds in 1963 his whole life plans were changed in a flash. His concentrated studies were not now as a future doctor but as an international pianist who had been rightly handed the key to unlock the door of success. Music means everything to him and since his initial success nearly two decades ago, not only has London and its main concert platforms seen him regularly with a full repertoire but he has travelled to most parts of the world, except South America and Australia and no doubt those will be visted ere long. He said his tours had been particularly enjoyable in the Far East, especially Hong Kong and Singapore. From my knowledge of these fascinating places it would have been thrilling to hear him play Beethoven's 'Emperor' concerto in any of these settings. Beethoven, as with most leading pianists, occupies a high place in his repertoire and is a favourite composer along with Mozart. Not unexpectedly for one who must value and take the greatest care of his hands, physical sports do not interest. He was grateful that he did not have to participate in military National Service. It would of course have been undertaken but with reluctance as an interference in, to him, matters more meaningful.

'What are your hobbies, then?'

'I love listening to music and visiting the theatre. When any friend is playing they are made doubly enjoyable. I'm fond too of walking in every part of the Lake District—a wonderful spot. To me it is music in physical form. I never, never tire of it.'

'Music in physical form'. What a perfect description of some of England's most glorious soul-satisfying scenery. My mind went back to a friend's opinion of the sunset behind Bowfell and the head of the Langdales as viewed from Orrest Head— '*the* view in all Britain which should not be missed'. Michael Roll had summed it up unforgettably.

I asked if he had any secret for success and he answered as I had anticipated. 'I do not like the word 'success'. It depends what you mean by it. If you are talking of career success, even financial success, I am just not interested. Artistic success—yes, that does mean something. Perfectionist expression in my playing—yes. Trying to achieve that is the thing that makes all the hard work and travelling worth-while.'

'Any advice to youngsters at the outset of their careers?'

'Yes, I think I would say be self-critical. Always have a whole-hearted approach to whatever job you are called upon to do. Graft your enthusiasm to modesty. I can think of no better counsel to give them.' The concert world will for a long time to come hear much of Michael Roll. Leeds, although he now lives in Buckinghamshire, will continue to have a civic pride in his achievements. A charming quiet spoken gentleman full of gentleness and humility.

Henry Moore is sculptor-extraordinary, the doyen of sculptors, a legend in his own lifetime. We are told that he was born at 36, Roundhill Road, Castleford on 30th July 1898 *the son of a miner.* There is no disputing the date of his birth but 'the son of a miner' gives a misleading impression and does not do justice to Henry's father, for he was no orthodox miner. If he had been fortunate enough to have had education of the type available to children of today, Moore senior would have quickly risen to the top of the mining profession. Although he was in the pit for a time, he quickly pulled himself out by tenacity which is a characteristic trait of a Yorkshireman. Self-taught he mastered mathematics and technical knowledge and succeeded as a mining engineer, which is rather different from the miner conjured up in our imagination. We include Henry Moore in this compendium of local celebrities because notwithstanding that he was born in nearby Castleford, he laid the foundation for the art of sculpting at the Leeds College of Art, but perhaps even to say that is to rush ahead.

Henry was one of eight children and he received just the right sort of encouragement from a wise, clear thinking and far-sighted father. To him, to his headmaster at Castleford Grammar School and to its art mistress, who made it clear that there was more to education than passing examinations, he owes a great deal. It was on visits, taken under her supervision, to Kirkstall Abbey that he first met art forms in the open, and to Methley church, where its stone heads awakened the interest that was to be later expressed in his sculptures. He was only about ten or eleven when this first love was aroused and it intensified his pleasure in the drawing lessons. Outside school he experimented carving bits of wood and even tried his hand on odd pieces of stone. He has told of a Sunday school teacher relating a story about 'the greatest sculptor in the world' and it stuck in his mind. From that time forth he knew he too wanted to be a sculptor. He spent a lot of his spare time visiting the Yorkshire churches that were accessible from his home with the one object of studying the sculptures they contained. When his father learnt of his eagerness to earn his livelihood as a sculptor he reacted as the wise counsellor and put forward true Yorkshire prudence. 'Alright, Henry so be it......But don't you think it would be a good idea to qualify as a schoolteacher so that if anything goes wrong you will at least have something on which to fall back?"

He acquiesced to father's suggestion and in 1915 became a student-teacher and a year later returned to his boyhood elementary school but this time as a member of the staff. The war did not allow him to pursue his scholastic career for long. In 1917 he joined the Army and was gassed at Cambrai. His health was so affected that he could not return to the battle area and was appointed a physical training instructor before being demobilized in February 1919.

And this is where Leeds steps into the picture. As an ex-service man he was eligible for a place as a college student and he secured entry to the Leeds School of Art for the September term of 1919. His natural ability was so encouraged and trained there that three years later he won a scholarship to the Royal College of Art in London. The influence in Leeds in span of time had been short but in terms of the outstanding success of his future career it had been immeasurable.

He has referred to his 'horrible little room in his digs in Sydney Street'—but his sojourn in London proved well worthwhile. Sir William Rothenstein was head of the college; he had a tradition of inviting one or two students to his home on Sunday evenings and there they had the opportunity of not only discussing art but of broadening their outlook by meeting other leaders in various fields. Poet Walter de la Mare and Ramsay Macdonald were guests he met at Sir William's—what foresight for a Principal to offer students the chance to mingle with well-known personalities! There was one aspect of the college work which he abhorred—'an affliction' he termed it—when each month students' work was pinned on a wall and criticised by a senior member of the staff. One of his early 'pin-up' contributions was tersely dismissed in a sentence—'That young man has been feeding on garbage.' Nevertheless, after a Royal College of Art training, the young artists and sculptors emerged knowing full well that 'the supreme question about a work of art is out of how deep a life does it spring'.

Henry Moore was appointed in 1924 as assistant in the sculpture department of the college with the opportunity of using a travelling scholarship in Italy. A great period of creation followed and the three-dimensional Reclining Figure, one of his most ambitious attempts of 1929, came to the Leeds Art Gallery. In 1930 he completed no less than twenty sculptures which proves fertility of mind and hard physical graft by any standards.

Moore was a loner, a solitary force, who found an advocate in Sir Herbert Read. It was Sir Herbert who realised the potential genius of Moore and was not slow in voicing abroad that he was one of a group of young artists revitalising British art. Like so many who had perforce to deviate from their habitual life, the war years were sculptually barren from 1940-43 but he was appointed war artist and used this post to set down an impression of those primitive nights in London's Underground stations at the height of the bombings. The drawings were masterpieces, Belsen-like in execution and stark in their fierceness and realism. He followed these with a series depicting an environment that he knew so well from boyhood and from his father's reminiscences—'Miners at the coal-face'. Leaving his sculptures aside, the 'Tube' and the 'Pit' sketches rank as great Moore work. In 1945, he stepped on to the pinnacle and has remained there ever since—the Englishman whose name is the first spoken when contemporary art is considered. He became an accepted public figure of world renown and it was said of him that 'he was to art what Winston Churchill was to public affairs'.

This Leeds-cum-Castleford son will be ever remembered for his majestic carvings—reclining figures, mother and child, family groups—which revealed vision and a vehicle for the emotions. The layman may have found it difficult to understand some of his creations. Some indeed have gone so far as to reject them, but he is confident that future generations will assimilate them easily and gladly. He adds, 'Sculpture is an art of the open air. Daylight, sunlight is necessary to it, and for me its best setting and complement is nature'.

In 1955 he was made a Companion of Honour and in 1963 he received the Order of Merit. He is now living in a village in Hertfordshire—not only living but still working! In September 1980 he stood beside the Environment Secretary, Michael Heseltine, in Kensington Gardens to watch the unveiling of 'The Arch', a 19 foot high sculpture carved in marble which he has given for permanent display on the north bank of Long Water.

Let us leave Henry Moore on a more personal and family note. In 1972 when packing and crating for a major exhibition of his sculptures made it impossible for him to work in his studios, he retreated to a small studio overlooking a field and pondered on the sheep he saw. He made some vigorous sketches of the animals—he said that he had always liked sheep because they belonged to the landscapes of his Yorkshire boyhood. Originally he gave the sketch-book of sheep to his daughter, Mary, and now it has been published in book form.

Margaret Storm Jameson was a novelist whose roots were grounded in the soil of Leeds University, but was a transplant there from North-East Yorkshire. She was born in Whitby on 8th January 1891 (and still happily with us), the daughter of a sea-captain, William Storm Jameson. He was fond of taking his wife to sea when he set sail on long voyages and consequently Margaret often found herself boarded out with certain Misses Corney. In 1907 mother pointed out that three county scholarships to University were awarded on the results of matriculation examinations, and in suggesting that she tried for one also indicated that her chances of success would be increased if she journeyed daily to the Municipal School at Scarborough. The advice proved fruitful and she was awarded a 'County' for Leeds University. Apart from childhood days with the Corneys it was her first taste of life away from home.

In those days there was no hostel for the women undergraduates and she took private accommodation with varying degrees of satisfaction with her choices. She moved lodgings four times in two years and in each her only favourable comment was that she was within minutes of *running* time to her lectures and that she was free to come and go as she pleased. For those benefits she was prepared to overlook dingy bedrooms and meagre suppers. In spite of her near proximity to the University, she missed many literary lectures but seems to have found no difficulty in graduating with honours. She has told how, in writing a thesis of 80,000 words on William Blake for her degree, she spent the whole of July and August at the Leeds Public Library in stifling heat, suffering from a fever for a fortnight of this period. She had Yorkshire grit without a doubt. One of her memories of saying farewell to Leeds is of leaving behind a debt of £15 owing to a bookseller—a debt which took her four years to repay. Her talents at the University did not go unrecognised. She was awarded the John Rutson research scholarship to University College, London, real help in her writing career, but like so many would-be authors she found that first time—or even second or third time—acceptances by publishers were the exception rather than the rule.

Few writers are usually so honest as Storm Jameson. She has declared, 'I am not what you call a born writer and I should have been much happier as an engineer....My earliest novels are not very good.' Few critics would wish to dispute an authoress' own judgment.

She married Guy Chapman, the publisher and author and again is frank about her housewifery abilities: 'I am a fine self-taught cook. I detest the heat of the oven, it makes me swear like a third mate, and I touch greasy pans as I would a viper, with loathing. I darn beautifully—sometimes when I watch it darning, my finger is my father's long-finger. I have all his physical patience, and a metaphysical impatience of the devil.' From 1933 onwards her novels were increasingly concerned with the state of the world, the mystery of treachery and cruelty. She revealed herself as an outspoken anti-Nazi and a hardworking friend of writers fleeing from Hitler's tyranny. In money matters she dramatically describes herself as 'incontinent'—a masterpiece of the laconic.

She was a naturally gay person, when not harassed by responsibilities and loved the theatre, opera, ballet and films. She once remarked that she would have sought these forms of amusement every evening of the week if she had had the opportunity. She was passionately fond of travel and again could never have her fill. Perhaps it was the blood of her sea-captain father flowing through her veins, but no other sensual or intellectual pleasure gave her a fraction of the acute happiness of visiting a foreign city. There was a restlessness about her which dominated her and which could be assuaged by no other means than travel. Even her novels which brought her fame—and there were so many that did just that—did not bring her that inward satisfaction that flowed from foreign travel. She made hundreds of friends in the course of her wanderings abroad and at home—Leeds is glad that she passed through the city and tarried awhile many years ago.

One of my boyhood memories is of eagerly looking each morning at the *Leeds Mercury* to see if my date of birth was listed among about a dozen other birthdays. If it was (and it did happen just once) then, on making a claim, I would be rewarded by a gift to delight any schoolboy's eye—something attractive and definitely not tawdry. This is probably the appropriate time to have a glance at a famous editor of the *Mercury* who helped fashion a merger with the *Yorkshire Post* and who is a notable 'giant' of the immediate past, having died as recently as 1972. Of course, W.L.A., the pseudonym of **Sir William Linton Andrews**. After early education in

Hull, and London, he had journalistic posts in many parts of Britain before seeing *really* active service with the Black Watch Regiment in World War I. His blood tingling despatches from the front line, especially on the occasions of the big battles, caught the imagination of the public and the eye of Lord Northcliffe. It was a natural step after demobilisation in 1919 to join the staff of the *Daily Mail* but after Northcliffe's death he was unsettled and gladly accepted the editorship of the *Leeds Mercury*. He was astonished to find the cramped Leeds office in New Station Street a breeding ground for indiscipline, with his orders antagonistically interpreted and disobeyed. 'I knew the discipline of war', wrote Shakespeare. W.L.A. said he would know the discipline of peace......in the *Mercury* office. It was a battle soon won and the paper took up again its traditions of campaigning for local causes and wider issues.

We recall that W.L.A.'s leader played a definite part in starting the 1936 abdication crisis of Edward VIII. This is not the place to re-cap in full that emotion-rousing saga but Sir John Baillie, Vice-Chancellor of Leeds University, had said, 'It used to be part of our written constitution that the King can do no wrong. That is no longer true.' W.L.A. quoted these words and fired the opening shot. The London press could no longer restrain itself and the fuse leading to the abdication was lit. The power of the spoken word plus the power of the Press.

On 26 November 1939 the *Mercury* was amalgamated with the *Yorkshire Post*, the latter retaining the main title but with W.L.A. sitting in the editorial chair. Blitzes—or quarter-blitzes as apparently they were officially termed—did not stop the old *Mercury* in its new guise. W.L.A. had his own correspondent with the 'D' Day Normandy landings; he had personal interviews with the great Winston and later 'Monty'. He says in his autobiography that 'he never expected bright success or public honours but I was given a knighthood, an Honorary Doctorate of Law at Leeds, elected a patron of Leeds Parish Church, took the first steps that revived the Leeds Triennial Musical Festival, and edited a book—*The Yorkshire Post: Two Centuries*.' He died on 27 September 1972.

Our last look in this brief miniature is at the moment of his retirement from his editorship. W.L.A. was honoured with a printer's farewell salute never before accorded to an editor. He received a printer's jerry. Everyone in the case room took hold of a mallet to bang on the 'turtles'—moveable tables to hold pages of type—or on any other metal surface that was handy. It is with such enthusiastic din that printers welcome an apprentice as he emerges from his articles, the birth of a first child, or the New Year. The compliment to one outside the craft—a mere editor!—was the exception that proves that a bond of fellowship *can* be forged between master and man that goes deeper than material gain.

Richard Hoggart is a local boy who has risen to a place of eminence in the world of literature and education. We now look at Hoggart's earliest days to appreciate just how far he has gone along the road of success.

He was born on 24th September 1918 at 48, Potternewton Lane, Chapeltown. The area was partly hemmed in by working class terraced houses, but immediately in front of No. 48 was a field in which he recalls as a boy of five seeing a cow calve......and that only a mile and a half from the city centre. He mentioned that the house itself had a living room, a scullery at the back with a single cold tap. The stairs rose out of the living room that had a big old-fashioned range. There was a room over the living room and a smaller one over the scullery. 'That's where my mother and the three children—I had a brother and sister—lived. There was an outside lavatory with an earth closet.'

His father had been a soldier; he died about 1921 and from then on his mother was looking after the family on her own. Most of the time she was tired and ill. They were living wholly on public assistance. His mother drew a small amount of money from the Board of Guardians but was given part of it in the form of coupons which had to be spent at specified shops. Their food was as basic as it could be. Tinned cocoa and condensed milk at about three (old) pence a tin. If mother wanted to keep her children quiet for a while she would give them a half slice of bread with a bit of margarine and some condensed milk on it. Unfortunately Mrs Hoggart had chest trouble and consequently was unable to earn extra money.

She only survived her husband by a few years and, the family being split amongst relatives, Richard was sent to his grandmother's home. Again he was just over a mile from the city centre but south of the river, in Hunslet in a house set amongst row after row of the same symmetrical dirty red-brick back-to-back houses, with cobbled streets, corner shops and a Board school. His grandma's house had an attic—1s 6d more in rent each week than the neighbours—with a bath and a clothes-horse screen for privacy. He slept in that attic—and if a neighbour's daughter was getting married they would seek permission for her to have a pre-marital bath......in Richard's bedroom!

He enjoyed his schooling in his Potternewton days and he would have been about seven or eight when he went to school in Hunslet—Jack Lane Council School. He has painful memories of his early days at the school. It was a slum school. He was beaten by the inevitable school bully for, as he put it, 'talking posh'. He had his first taste of anti-semitism. The bully decided that he was a Jew—which was untrue—and would persist in calling him 'Sheeny' and hitting him. 'Jack Lane' was surprisingly a 'boys only' school and the headmaster was, of necessity, tough, but he had the foresight to see that young Hoggart was a bright lad and had the patience and the will to develop what he thought he saw. The morning he took his scholarship examination he walked the lengthy distance to Cockburn School to sit the paper. 'Jack Lane' did not specially prepare for scholarships as Ernest Woodroofe's school had done, and Richard failed, but his headmaster was a dedicated man, and on hearing the result, wasted no time in approaching the hierarchy in the local education offices. 'Look at that boy's essay. Can't you see there's talent in it?' That was his opening gambit and the final shots brought about a change in the original decision. Young Hoggart went to Cockburn.

As has already been remarked, Cockburn had a staff with a sense of mission. He told me that he remembered well Peaker, Milner, and Champion, who had so conscientiously served Woodroofe; along with Deakin, a Latin master who taught him a lot about keeping one's head down and going at it. He found Cockburn a curiously interesting school and realised later that by the time you had gone through the hoops of furious competition to get there you were either very good indeed or you had enormous staying power.... or luck. The headmaster of the time he described as 'an odd character'. He came from Dulwich College and left to enter an Anglican monastery. In the Cockburn spell sandwiched between, however, he gave Hoggart his first sight of a mind speculating; of thought as something disinterested and free-playing, with himself outside it. Cockburn's headmaster was one key person and later, a second was Professor Dobrée of Leeds University.

I did my homework at the end of the kitchen table. I don't remember getting the idea of going forward to higher education. I did what I was told to do, one step after another. I didn't have a vision of a goal. I enjoyed doing the work. I did four years to matriculation during which time I had one nervous breakdown. At least I've been able to cope with my worst situations since. After I took a very good "matric" the Board of Guardians visitor persuaded them to increase my allowance to my grandmother from 7s 6d to 15s a week and on this she felt I could go ahead.'

He worked for Higher School Certificate—'A' levels of today but necessitating a composite pass. He was rewarded with one out of the total of twenty Senior City scholarships Leeds gave that year and with this went to the English Department at Leeds University—Oxford or Cambridge did not seem to have been suggested at that time. To be one of twenty out of a city population of nearly half-a-million was a glimpse of the genius which lay ahead. He went to university in a mixed state of mind. Enthusiastic, keenly interested but with a knowledge that he did not have enough money to do anything special. After his week's simple necessities were met he had 1s 6d left for pocket money. Think of it—7½p in 1982 money. As he rightly said, 'You couldn't cut a dash on that even in the '30s, but I wasn't the only one by any means.'

Looking back from that moment of time he summed it up, 'There were several major turning points in my childhood. The move to my grandmother's home. The scholarship exam at eleven. In terms of personalities: my grandmother, the headmaster of the secondary school and Bonamy Dobrée.'

Bonamy Dobrée was about forty-five when Hoggart first came under his influence as a 'promising student'. At the beginning of his third year Dobrée started to pay personal attention to him—he was included in the circle who were loosely under his wing. Hoggart wanted to risk 'mental congestion' and to read psychology as a new supplementary subject—but his mentor had a clear sense of the danger of overstudy. Richard Hoggart continued on the single path of English Literature. There was practical help too from Dobrée. He knew of his protege's impecuniousness—his grandmother had died and he was living in a University hostel and finding it difficult to make ends meet—and personally arranged for the Registrar to make him a welcome extra grant. He left Bonamy Dobrée with an Arts degree (later to return to complete his Doctorate of Literature), and conscious of the necessity of the qualities his leader had shown him—hardwork and thoroughness, a detailed attention to whatever job was in hand, a touch of the happy warrior, a refusal to sentimentalise, a kind of stiff dignity, courtesy and magnanimity.

Hoggart married Mary France in 1942, whilst serving with the Royal Artillery from which he was demobilised as a Staff Captain. He spent six years in the Forces and returned to be a tutor at Hull University followed by several university appointments leading to the Assistant Directorship of the United Nations Educational, Scientific and Cultural Organisation in Paris—UNESCO. For five years, until 1975, he performed this role and was by now internationally famous. He had already been invited to deliver in 1971 the annual series of Reith lectures for the B.B.C.

Now, as Warden of Goldsmiths' College of the University of London, doubtless further honours will come his way. In all his work he has drawn much from his boyhood experiences, portraying in masterly style and fascinating detail the working class of North England, and of Leeds in particular. No more absorbing and important work on the life of this group in Hunslet, fathers, mothers, sisters and brothers, has been published than his book *The Uses of Literacy*, whilst amongst his many other writings his studies and research on W.H. Auden is acknowledged as authoritative. He is currently engaged on writing his autobiography. When that eventually emerges from the presses it will be compulsive reading. No better 'loiner' than Richard could wind up this commentary on those who have touched the local Arts scene at one point or another in their lives.

5. The World of Entertainment

Willis Hall—Keith Waterhouse—Peter O'Toole—Jimmy Savile—Frankie Vaughan—R.C. Sriven

THE world of entertainment........in Leeds. Boyhood memories come cascading back. The Grand Theatre pantomime, the glittering spectacular show—but the old Theatre Royal, where now Schofields will sell you anything from finery to furniture, was the more personally attractive because the comedians seemed more to my Yorkshire taste. Reg. Bolton or Albert Modley as Buttons, the butt of the charming 'Laidler's Little Sunbeams', schoolgirl dancers who captured everyone's heart. What a feast in store as you sat in the uppercircle, envied the dress circle below and scorned the gallery above.

When the Paramount Cinema was opened, at the junction of Briggate and the Headrow, what a delight to step into the foyer, sink almost ankle deep in a pale blue and beige carpet, on your way to the most luxurious armchair seat a Leeds picture palace had offered its patrons. To know that at least three hours of fantasy was in front, with a break for the personal appearance of a guest star, and enlivened by the organist rising as if on a lift but really astride the 'Mighty Wurlitzer'.

What a queue outside the Rialto, opposite Woolworths, when Al Jolson 'sang' in 'The Singing Fool'. 'Talkies' had come to town to become the talk of the town. And the dance enthusiasts were not forgotten. The Majestic and the Mecca-Locarno Ballrooms catered for their tastes. The Empire, the Hippodrome, the City Varieties and the old Queen's Theatre in Holbeck were there for those who loved the music-halls for the magic and the fun they provided.

In those days my youthful mind felt that Leeds must be one of the centres of the entertainment world, even if it could not be *the* hub. And now, I find that some who have graced this sphere of pleasure and make-believe were sons and daughters of the city, either indigenous or temporary, but all with an association not to be overlooked.

Paradoxically, the first whom we shall meet are neither stage nor film stars but dramatists and writers whose productions have been seen in theatres on both sides of the Atlantic, on cinema screens throughout the world, on television, on radio, whilst novels and regular newspaper columnist contributions have made up their more than full-work load. We must consider this pair together—the twinning of their names comes automatically to one's mind—**Willis Hall** and **Keith Waterhouse**.

Their achievements are staggering. If ever it can be true to use that oft quoted and often meaningless phrase, 'It is impossible to give a complete list of published work', now is the time. Keith's novels include *Billy Liar, There is a Happy Land, Jubb, The Bucket Shop* and he has worked extensively with his friend, Willis, following their outstandingly successful collaboration on the stage production of *Billy Liar*. For the theatre they have jointly written *Celebration, England our England, All Things Bright and Beautiful* and many others, and have adapted from an Italian work *Saturday Sunday, Monday* (which gained for them a 'Best Play of the Year' award). Their work in films and television is equally as numerous and successful.

Having written so many stage plays and other offerings in the past quarter of a century they are regarded as the standby professionals of the British theatre. To refer to them, coming from a cricketing county, as the 'Hobbs and Sutcliffe' partnership of the stage would be most apposite and for quality of craftsmanship just as true, their technical skill never in doubt. Willis Hall's *The Long and the Short and the Tall*, premiered in 1958, was presented the following year at the Royal Court Theatre with another Leeds associate, Peter O'Toole, in a part which he accepted with enthusiasm and used as a step on his own pathway to fame.

Just some of their triumphs of stage, screen—large and small—and books. But what manner of men are these, Leeds born and bred. Firstly, when I wanted to find out, in some depth, I could never have been greeted with more friendliness and more willing co-operation than they accorded me. It was Willis Hall who said, 'With regard to my early life, I've no idea how much or how little you need to know, but I'm sure we can solve it together.' Keith said, 'I am just going away and scrambling to finish my work-load. I hope what I can tell you will be adequate.' From these helpful responses it was not difficult to learn much of their backgrounds.

Purely by chance my contact was with Willis Hall first. He was born in Leeds on 6th April 1929, lived in the 'Addingtons', a complex of terraced houses off Dewsbury Road and went to nearby Cockburn School. Willis left school at fourteen but remembers without hesitation one person there: 'My personal claim to Old Cockburnian fame is that I sat in the next desk to the lady destined to be Mrs Frankie Vaughan—Stella Shock!'

'After leaving Cockburn, I spent three months as an apprentice deck-hand on a trawler—believe me, it seemed much longer.' When asked what were the duties of an 'apprentice deck-hand', he replied laconically—'Everything.'

He left the sea for the well-known 'Yorkshire Relish' firm, had a spell with the *Yorkshire Evening News* and then joined the Royal Corps of Signals as a professional soldier—'Five years with the Colours and seven on the Reserve.' He was posted to the Far East for a considerable period. Radio Malaya wanted a playwright for their Chinese Schools Department and he landed the job! This, together with work on the Forces radio there, taught him a great deal about the craft of script-writing and he proved an apt pupil. He had been friendly with Keith Waterhouse since his boyhood—they were both about the same age and collaboration with him followed naturally on his return to England and civilian life.

I knew he had written extensively about sport and having been born within cheering distance of the home of Hunslet Rugby League club felt sure he would have some memories of Parkside. 'Of course, I often went down the ginnel to it. What Hunslet lad didn't find his way into Parkside? I knew Jack Walkington (an excellent full-back and coach) and Ted Carroll—the expert in being the most surprised person on the field when singled out for the ref's special blessing! Eddie Waring was at Headingly of course but I was with him in his "Evening News" days. I've written though more especially of soccer and am a director of Brentord F.C.'

The secret of his success? 'Sticking at it, whatever that "it" is. And I would give the same advice to any youngster trying to get a toehold as a scriptwriter or actor—"STICK AT IT".'

Willis seemed to be expressing the same sentiments about dramatists and playwrights.... and about other walks of life, too. The number of plays and novels he has written indicate how thoroughly he has carried out his recommendation—it is as impressive a work-load as friend Waterhouse.

I wondered which part of his writing did he enjoy most, writing novels or writing for the stage or television screen. 'I have no favourites. I enjoy doing them all. You see—I enjoy writing.... just writing.'

And hobbies! 'Give me a soccer or a rugger match and I'm happy.'

Keith Spencer Waterhouse was born at Low Road, Hunslet, on 6th February 1929. The family soon moved to Bestbrooke Street and when he was four to Middleton Park Grove. He told me that he went to school at the John Blenkinsop Middle School and at the age of ten when his family moved, to Halton Moor Estate, to Osmondthorpe School. When a television film was made of his novel *There is a Happy Land* he had some scenes shot at his old school at Middleton. He had eighteen months at the Leeds College of Commerce, having been awarded a commercial scholarship, but actually his entry into the commercial field had occurred at a much earlier age! In 1939 he 'worked' a newspaper round and recalls that with each copy of the *Yorkshire Post* or whatever paper he had to push through the letter-boxes he also put through a copy of his own 'newspaper' which he had grandiosely titled 'The Daily Treasure'. As a boy he was connected with Mill Hill chapel in City Square, and tells of the attraction there which much appealed to him. It had a very flourishing youth club. He was a journalist for four years from 1948 on the editorial staff of the *Yorkshire Evening Post*.

'What were you doing between leaving school and joining the "Post"?'

'I worked first at J.T. Buckton and Sons—estate agents *and* undertakers (!) in New Station Street.' (Billy Liar must have been pure nostalgic Buckton's, but I forgot to ask him outright.) 'I was then called up for National Service in the Royal Air Force and returned to journalism on the Yorkshire Evening Post.'

Whilst he was a reporter on the *Evening Post* he undertook to walk to London—covering about thirty miles a day—and wrote a series of articles on his journey. 'Having liked what I saw of London while trudging via High Wycombe I came to Fleet Street.' He now has his popular *Daily Mirror* column.

'Have you any pet dislikes?' There was no mistaking his single gun-fire reply—'Snobs'.

And the 'success' question which I find most intriguing when put to those whose names are household words. He re-iterated unknowingly Willis Hall's recipe by summing it up as 'Hard work'. He is certainly living that out. He continued, 'If any young man or young woman would wish to write successfully for the stage then they really should involve themselves with the local theatre—local radio and so on. All are stepping stones, all hold the keys to future success.'

It is time to say farewell to these 'loiners' who have travelled far in the world of entertainments. Having learnt at first hand something of them, I realised that they had taken a Yorkshire town, written naturally and frankly of life at the working class level, and married them on to their own early backgrounds. They equally as well could reflect on life in the upper crust of London's Society, or war in Malaya. They see life and write of what they see. They are a grand pair ready to extend a hand to those who seek their help.

It was Keith Waterhouse who advised becoming involved in the local theatre. **Peter O'Toole** did just that.... at the Civic Theatre in the Leeds' Albert Hall in Cookridge Street when he made his first stage appearance in 1949, at the age of seventeen. Before that he had tried his hand as a budding journalist in the photographic department of the *Yorkshire Evening News*—the newspaper with which Willis Hall and Eddie Waring were both associated. The editor told him frankly, and no doubt helpfully, that he would never make a newspaper man and recommended his trying to earn a living in some other way. Perhaps though we should go back to the beginning of the story.

Peter O'Toole was born in Ireland on 2nd August 1932 but his father, a bookmaker, emigrated to Leeds—to the Hunslet area of Willis Hall and Keith Waterhouse—and part of his education was gained at the Roman Catholic St. Annes School. After his National Service and thinking over his former editor's advice he decided to re-develop an earlier love, his schoolboy interest in amateur theatricals. On demobilisation he applied to the Royal Academy of Dramatic Art and was awarded a scholarship. He followed this with a three year theatrical apprenticeship at the Bristol Old Vic and did not waste his time—he had more than seventy parts, ranging from Shakespeare to pantomime, in that triennial spell. By 1959 he had been appearing in London for two years and he gave a performance of Private Bamforth in Willis Hall's *The Long and the Short and the Tall* which earned for him the 1959 Best Actor of the Year award. Turning down film offers he joined the Royal Shakespeare Company for a season at Stratford-on-Avon to have the opportunity presented by the leading roles in their repertoire. In 1962 he shot to film stardom with the title role in *Lawrence of Arabia* and his striking facial resemblance combined with superlative acting brought him international fame. He made further films year by year, giving outstanding performances even if some of the material in which he had to work was trivial. In 1965 the West End play in which he was appearing—*Ride a Cock Horse*—was a failure so he decided to turn his back on the London stage and thereafter trod the boards in Bristol, Dublin and America. But even changes of venue brought him ups and downs; success and failure. At the Dublin Festival in 1976 *Dead Eye Dicks*, a play that he had sponsored himself, was denounced by the critics, and having done so badly in the provinces, it never reached the West End as the vehicle in which he intended to make his London come-back.

After fifteen years he returned to the capital and the man once hailed as the new Olivier stepped out as Macbeth at the theatre which saw him in 1963—the Old Vic. He felt it to be the right moment to come in a dual capacity of actor and Associated Director of the Old Vic, to set the seal of success on a new phase of his career. Has he achieved it? On the first night he took one of the most savage hammerings from the critics that the London theatre could remember. He was reported to have commented: 'This is supposed to be a blood-soaked failure. But the box-office is sold out. Can that be so bad? What did Henry Irving say: "No audience, no art". It has not been a recent custom in the British theatre for an actor in Shakespeare to be front page news or for the whole town to have on its lips but one topic of theatrical conversation......but that is what O'Toole achieved and I feel he has played his hand deliberately, that he will always be in demand and when he next portrays a character will have transformed the critics from an abusive pack to a wildly cheering mob. Peter O'Toole has shown genius in the past, he has shown it now if we look in depth at the 1980 Macbeth and he will certainly show it again in the future.

The name of the next Leeds celebrity is on millions of lips daily and has been for a long time. None other than **Jimmy Savile.......** O.B.E. The secret of his success is found in his kindly consideration for others; it shows in everything he undertakes. Busy man that he is, when I told him of my researches for this book he took the trouble to write me in his own hand—script not typewritten. He had just completed Jim's 'Daily Dozen' (Run-Walk-Stagger-Limp)—thirty one towns and cities in thirty-one days for the whole month of October 1979. As he rightly described it, 'A never-before type sponsored charity walk'.

I also approached someone who was well-acquainted with his voluntary services at Leeds General Infirmary, where his hospital portering duties are too well known to require repetition here. He told me that Jimmy had promised to open the Day Room at St. George's Hospital, Rothwell, and it unfortunately coincided with the day of his mother's funeral. His mother was the real love in his life and the bond of affection between them was deep and real. 'The Duchess' was how he referred to her. Rather than disappoint anyone, staff and patients alike, he had come straight from the funeral service at Scarborough to perform the opening. 'The very fact that he did it was a remarkable thing, and his speech revealed his passionate concern for the elderly and his down-to-earth knowledge of their day-to-day problems.' The other recollection my friend had of Jimmy Savile was his willing support to the campaign to ensure that the new extension to the Leeds Infirmary was built.... at a time when there was great danger that the project might be cancelled.

Jimmy is Leeds to the core and from the age of four to fourteen was a pupil, along with Peter O'Toole, at St. Annes School, where he received a thorough grounding in the Catholic faith which has remained with him. But from those schooldays has emerged a flamboyant figure, a personality created by the mass media phenomena of the age. It is no fault of Jimmy Savile that his stardom brings with it the Midas touch but it is to his everlasting credit that he has fully shared his affluence with many. To be paid £50,000 in 1974 for a thirty minute appearance at the Ideal Homes Exhibition in London is a commentary on this current mad reign of Mammon; his handling of this fee is to see his true profile—he gave it to the Stoke Mandeville Hospital for paralytic cripples.

From the age of eleven, long before he left St. Annes, his life story is of a multitude of facets bubbling over with ceaseless activity—the human equivalent of perpetual motion. Each picture follows its predecessor like beads tightly threaded on a string.

At eleven, calling at the Mecca Dance Hall, off Briggate, after school to find out if he was wanted for a session to play on the drums. If he was lucky, sunny Jim was better off by ten shillings. Worth having in those wartime days. At fourteen, office boy at fifteen shillings a week—a little wonder that a drummer-boy's pay seemed wealth.

As a teenager he rode in a Tour of Britain cycle race—he continued his love of the sport by cycling in 1973, for charity, from Land's End to John O'Groats. Incidentally he also did this lengthy stretch on foot on another occasion, giving him a notable 'double'. When his turn came for National Service, his name came out of the Government hat of Ernest Bevin for the coal-mines. He was a Bevin boy posted to South Kirby Colliery for four years and obtained first hand knowledge of the discomforts and dangers of the coal face. For a lengthy part of this period he had the monotonous job of watching the coal tubs pass a certain point to see that they did not come off the track. Rather like counting sheep in uncomfortable circumstances but with equally soporific effect. To offset any feeling of drowsiness he did a sensible thing—he put his time to good use by mildly academic studies of a general nature.

He was transferred to Waterloo Colliery, nearer to his home in Leeds, but it was a move to an old pit where he had no time for underground study—he found life much harder and tougher. He was injured in a shot-firing accident and was unable to continue at the colliery for many weeks. In Savilean fashion he did not waste this period of freedom. He hired a room at the Belle Vue Road branch of the Loyal Order of Ancient Shepherds, adjusted a gramophone to give him the volume he required and set up a 'disco'—a disc jockey had been born. His Bevin boy days came to an end, and to where he had once been a young drummer, he returned with the fine sounding title of assistant manager at a weekly wage of £8. His unorthodoxy, which seemed to be inbuilt in him, came to the front again—he lived on what had been a lifeboat, moored just below Leeds Bridge. Not exactly idyllic surroundings but most convenient for work. Mecca moved him about—Ilford, Manchester, back to Leeds. But he was still very much a routine manager—slight promotion by now but not sufficient to feed his ambitious appetite. How to lift himself out of the rut; how to be notorious? Jimmy found the answer. He dyed his hair blonde, and for good measure and for guaranteed results, followed it with other warmer coloured dyes. The teenagers flocked to his dance-hall now—he felt he must be amongst the world's best dance-hall managers when he saw the crowds. This was the real start of the rocket ride to fame. He was offered an opening as a disc-jockey with Radio Luxemburg; a weekly column followed in the *Sunday People* and then he found he was 'top of the pops' on television. He moved his mother, by now always known as 'The Duchess', from her Leeds home to a South

Cliff flat in Scarborough and whilst he had not arrived, as we know him to-day, he was on his way. Mecca were paying him £25 a week, but he could earn £300 on his day off, so it did not need his underground studies in the pit to reveal that a sensible man should quit the mundane for the highly lucrative spectacular. He quit. He put his greater abundance of leisure to good use. He offered himself as an unpaid hospital porter at the Leeds Infirmary and from then on has, whenever he possibly could, given them two days weekly service. There must be countless Leeds citizens whose short ride from ward to operating theatre has been made just that little easier with the guiding hands and quips of Jimmy.

His urge for publicity; his desire to keep himself in the news, to be talked about—all, to his mind, essential if the television bubble was not to burst—made him undertake several stunts that called for courage, strength and purposeful resolve. He did a session as a dustbin man on a Scarborough round and loved it when the teenage girls spotted him. He took the place of a horse between the shafts of a tram on Douglas promenade; on a slightly uphill section he nearly burst a blood-vessel. He flew, not with the Red Arrows but the Fleet Air Arm equivalent, the Diamonds—a nerve-wracking experience.

He has never liked giving advice to the many individuals and groups who have sought it. He feels that running his own life is difficult enough, but, generalising, he does say, 'You have got to be different to get on.' Jimmy Savile never spoke a truer word!

His O.B.E. is a source of real pride and deep comfort. Like all persons about to receive a national honour, he learnt about it in advance, with the usual 'sworn to secrecy' admonition. He could not sleep on the night he received the news. Some might have got up and made a cup of tea or poured out a second 'night-cap'. Not Jimmy. He went over to Leeds Infirmary and moved a corpse from a ward to the mortuary. His signature always contains 'O.B.E.' as a full-stop flourish. He believes in the old soldiers' motto about medals—'Win 'em and wear 'em'—and so where Jimmy goes, his O.B.E. also goes.

There is no denying that a man of his earning capacity who donates so much of his time, talent and treasure to charity is a man 'with a heart of gold'.

'Happiness', it has been said, 'is a bye-product of doing what you like'.

Frankie Vaughan must be a happy man. He was an excellent art student with a future with pen and brush but who loved singing and keenly wanted to be a professional singer. Backed by his wife, he satisfied his vocal ambitions and has never looked back. A Leeds boy, born Frank Ableson, he has never outgrown his love of his early home and his family. It is most surprising that an introvert timid boy,—so shy that if he was asked to sing at a family party would only do so if he could sing in the hall outside the lounge door; one who would sing in the Synagogue choir but always out of sight of the congregation—could become, on the stage, a complete extrovert—a 'sock it to 'em' singing star, as he has been described.

His first stage appearance was as an amateur at the Leeds Empire with a Leeds University Rag Revue—the highlight of the undergraduates' fund-raising activities for local charities. His 'Al Jolson's' number was a tremendous success and unknowingly the first step on the way to fame. His grandmother was a Russian-Jew and when she heard of his *succès fou* she said, 'You will be number one, someday.' Her 'number one', in the phonetics of a Russian, sounded 'number vaun' and from that moment he knew that if he did take up a singing career he could be no other but Frankie *Vaughan*.

Willis Hall has told us that his class room neighbour at Cockburn was Stella Shock, soon to become Mrs Frankie Vaughan. Stella knew how keen he was to go on the stage as a singer and she never urged him to consider something with more security. They married, and as singer with Nat Temple's Band at £9 a week, moved to a two roomed flat in an uninviting district of London, for which they were charged a weekly rent of £5. Not much left on which to live; life was tough for them both, but neither grumbled. They looked to the future—she knew she had hitched her wagon to a star—a singing star.

He prospered, his voice and personality saw to that, and he received the inevitable call to the cinema world. He was excellent with Anna Neagle in *Dangerous Years* but on the other side of the Atlantic felt he had not received all the help he might have done. He played opposite Marilyn Monroe and his family assert that that film spoilt his acting career. To Hollywood he was inexperienced and encouragement was not a strong point in the celluloid city. He knew the troughs of the entertainment world—but only for a short duration. He quickly regained popularity and the peaks with his stage career. Like so many of these entertainment idols his generosity is a bye-word. At the time when he had his own band, he brought them to the Capitol Cinema at Meanwood and put on a show for the benefit of Jewish ex-servicemen in the city. He launched in 1968—and it still continues—with the chief constable of Glasgow the Easterhouse Project, a social experiment to combat youth crime in the east end of Glasgow. His activities with the Lancaster Boys' Club are well known and these have their roots in his war-time associations with the county town. It was there, whilst his father was away in the Army, that his mother had a little corner shop.

It was when I was talking to Willis Hall that he said, 'Whoever you omit from your book, don't leave out **R.C. Scriven**—look at his life, he is both a poet and author, but is perhaps best known for his masterly radio plays.' Looking into his life unfolded a story of courage and craftsmanship. At the age of eight he contracted an ear infection that left him almost stone deaf and—later—was to make him blind. Yet so intensely were his years of hearing and of seeing vividly remembered that they became the well-spring of his working life both as a poet and radio dramatist. 'Drugged', he said, 'with a beauty I cannot see.' He had a command of language, the ability to paint a landscape in words that have won for him a unique reputation.

Not Leeds born but coming of a prosperous Leeds engineering family, he came to the city to a house in Sholebrook Avenue on his second birthday, having been born in Sheffield on 21st April 1907. His grandfather had founded the 'Leeds Old Foundry' in Jack Lane, Hunslet. Ronald Charles Scriven's father, John, had been sent to Sheffield as a consulting engineer and promised that on his eventual return to Leeds, he would be made a partner in the family business. Ronald's early schooling was at Miss Beal's Kindergarten adjoining Potternewton church, but those days in the Harehills Avenue district were curtailed when tragedy struck at the family. Early during the 1914-18 war his father had a nervous breakdown which developed into a permanent mental illness. With his mother and brother they moved into Ellers Road to live with grandmother Scriven. Still Fate had not done its worst. His mother too had a similar mental breakdown in 1916 and he and his brother were virtually orphans. The two boys experienced a tough·rough time fostered out to a farmer and his wife at North Rigton in Wharfedale. Farmer Robinson's wife, Ann, known as Iron Ann, taught him the meaning of discipline.

Scriven has described how, in the course of the first three days of the fostership, he was starved into submission to the will of Mrs Robinson. Young Ronald hated his porridge to be lumpy and refused to eat what Ann had put before him at his first breakfast. She set the same dish of cold porridge before him at dinner-time, the same cold porridge at tea-time; at supper-time.....it was still lumpy. The purgatory continued the next day—and the lad stuck it out; on the third day he stole a bit of food from the pig swill and carried on his defiance. But the fourth day was too much to bear, he caved in, was compelled to eat up the congealed glutinous mess. Ann had triumphed.

On the kitchen wall was a curious ornament. The front wheel brake of a bicycle, polished by the farmer's wife as a ritual every Saturday evening. Accidentally, on one occasion, Ronald knocked it from its hook, and was soundly thrashed—beyond reason for a trivial unintended offence. Only later did he learn that Ann's thirteen year old son had run away from home because he could not take her intolerable discipline. The front wheel brake was all she had with which to remember him.

He walked a mile and a half to school in the village and trudged back again at the end of the day. He took his dinner with him, usually a cold rice pudding which his foster mother had packed for him and his brother. The schoolmaster, with limited materials and in confined classroom space shared by scholars of varying ages, did a good job. What the ultimate result would have been is conjecture. He received news in March 1918 that his father had died and at the same time it was revealed to the Scriven boys that mother had died six months earlier. Real orphans now and to Crossley's School at Halifax they were sent. Ronald experienced a great deal of bullying but found refuge in reading, encouraged by his English master.

He matriculated well and set his sights on Oxford, but his guardian, Uncle James, who appears to have been the fly in the Scriven boys ointment for years, would hear nothing but a start for Ronald on the shop floor of the Jack Lane foundry, lodging with one of the workmen and his wife in Sebastopol Street. His heart was in literature not in engineering and after a series of blunders caused by this lack of interest his uncle handed him a farewell present of £10 and told him to make his own way in the world. Returning to Ellers Road and his grandmother, he wrote articles for a living and, in the evenings, poetry to satisfy his artistic leanings. Later his *The Year of the Phoenix and other poems* was published and highly acclaimed.

It was in his early fifties that he became blind through neglected glaucoma and writing from his sighted memories he achieved success as a radio dramatist. *A Single Taper* which told the story of an unsuccessful eye operation was hailed as a 'radio classic'. *The Seasons of the Blind* was commissioned by the B.B.C. for the Royal National Institute for the Blind's centenary and won him a Writers' Guild Award. David Wade, reviewing the play in *The Times,* wrote: 'I do not remember to have received in sound alone so vivid an impression of landscape; it was as if by some process of direct transmission the writers vision had been implanted in my brain.'

R. C. Scriven, writing of his affliction, said: 'There are only two things a man can do about a grievous disability. Put up with it or fold up. But Houseman said to me,

I won it in a weary land,
Wrung from a star that scored the hand.
But take it. If the brew be sour,
The better for the embittered hour.

My journey through the wasteland with such a companion made me, above all, one of their company.'

After those thoughts there is just nothing to add to the Scriven story except perhaps to say that happily he is still amongst us.

6. Sporting Celebrities

Geoff Gunney—Eddie Waring—Hedley Verity—Leonard Hutton

THERE are class divisions in Hunslet and in Headingley. North of the river the populace is divided into its support of Leeds United and Leeds Rugby club. South of the river, there are two classes equally as fiercely partisan. Those who would scorn New Hunslet R.L. club and those who cannot bring themselves to be seen queuing at the United ground. All turnstile sportsmen who lighten the worries of the shop-floor, the office desk, or the bus platform; who try to forget Mrs Thatcher, Michael Foot, Ronald Reagan, Leonid Ilyich Brezhnev, Uncle Tom Cobley and all by re-living in critical analysis last Saturday's, or in these anti-Sabbath days, Sunday's match.

For the moment, I am casting back to the old Hunslet whose song 'We've swept the seas before us and so we will again' echoed round the terraces of their home, Parkside; whose colours changed from chocolate and white to myrtle, flame and white but were always worn with a deep sense of loyalty born of a local spirit. From the hummock dividing Beeston Road from Dewsbury Road, from the Woodviews, the Trenthams, Lady Pit Lane, from all these terraced streets they drift in their ones, twos, and threes, past the New Inn past the Old Cresent Cinema, down the cinder track—"The Ginnel"—to click through the turnstiles ...... of Parkside. The flag is flying over the wooden pavilion. Hunslet are at home. This was in the days before the hooligans were loosed on the football scene; before it became a 'sport' to terrorise your fellow followers and the visitors' supporters: before it was necessary to send a posse of police instead of the solitary volunteer 'bobby' who sat ensconced in the touch-line straw, out for an afternoon's enjoyment—and paid for it. The days when the youngsters could safely go on their own, through the boys' entrance and in their jubilation, when Hunslet had touched down for a try, throw their caps into the air not caring where they descended. Before Hunslet were driven from home by the encroachment of factory development over well-nigh 'sacred' ground; before they had to find a new temporary home next door to their soccer friends, 'United', a home which even now has been denied them and left them as homeless refugees.

Hunslet has produced fine players—sporting celebrities of rare quality. We will look at one, **Geoffrey Gunney** M.B.E., whose record of loyalty to the club extends from 1951 to 1974—23 years for a forward in modern Rugby League is toughness and tenacity unsurpassed.

Geoff, for that is how all Hunslet knows him, was born on 9th November 1933 at Armley and was a pupil at Dewsbury Road County Primary School immediately behind the old and well-loved Pavilion Picture House. When I appraoched him to build up a pen picture of himself he was most affable and promised to help in any way possible. 'Ask me the questions, and if I know the answers I'll give them.'

'Tell me first something about your background and your family, Geoff.'

'Well grandfather Movley, on my mother's side, was one of the most successful track runners hereabouts. He ran for Harehills Harriers and was Northern Counties cross-country champion at ½-mile and 1,000 yards. I married Joyce in December 1957. She was a Sunbeam Terrace girl and we have a boy and a girl.'

He likes to tell a tale about his son, David, who played for the West Yorkshire under-15 R.L. team. 'I was down at Parkside. A ball was kicked into touch and a boy fielded it with expertise. An onlooker turned to me and remarked, "That lad is a natural. He certainly knows how to handle a rugby ball." He should do. He's my lad,' I replied.

'I was just nine years old when I played for Dewsbury Road school and I captained them when I was eleven. After that I went on to play for Hunslet schoolboys. Before that I fancied myself as a Leeds United player, but a pal told me all about Hunslet. It's hard to believe it today, but Hunslet players were better known than the United men. I switched my loyalties and from then on I made up my mind I would one day play for Hunslet. I suppose I was built for it, really, I was 6ft 1in at fifteen and weighted just over 13½ stones.'

After Geoff left school he was apprenticed to a heating engineer but since retiring from the game has been engaged in the motor trade. He first played for Hunslet on 10th May 1951 against Cardiff. Of the match he remembers trotting out as a nervous, ambitious and excited seventeen year old whose main claim in those days was as a goal-kicker. 'Well, I was lucky, landing two or three, I forget which, from difficult positions.'

He must have been the signing of the century—his signing on fee was £25! After six first team games he received another £25 and then on his 21st birthday a further £250. His contract also stipulated £50 for a Yorkshire 'cap' and £100 for playing for England. After just three 'A' team games, 'Bugs Bunny' as he had been nicknamed by his team-mates made that first team debut. Jack Walkington, the great Hunslet full-back who was then the team coach, must have sensed the potential of the lad because after only one more game with the second team he was in the first team again and there he stayed for 23 seasons and exactly 600 matches. When one thinks of any player staying in rugby for nearly a quarter of a century it is a magnificent achievement. But to stay with one club is a miracle. What a tribute to the loyalty of the 'gentle giant'. He could have secured better playing terms, more winning pay with the more fashionable clubs but nothing could persuade him to leave Parkside.

He first played for Yorkshire to earn his extra signing-on fee in 1955, but having played for England in 1954 he had already earned the £100 international bonus before his county one.

'How many caps altogether — Yorkshire and England?'

'Do you know, I can't answer that one, except by a lot of checking back through the old cuttings and so on. I know I had a junior England match in 1952 but as for the others I'll just settle for "I don't know".'

And likewise when I asked him how many goals he had kicked (and he was a leading goal-kicking specialist) and how many tries he had scored he just did not know. He never kept a score-card; he had never troubled to try to find out; he gave the impression that the thing that mattered was the game itself. However the story of one of his tries was told by an old friend, Jeff Stevenson, an international scrum-half who played for Leeds, York and later Hunslet.

'Geoff Gunney and his wife used to come over to my house on a Friday evening and there was always a lot of cross-talk when Hunslet played Leeds the next day. The particular match of which I am thinking, just before the kick-off, I went over to Geoff and shook hands, saying "All the best, Geoff and don't forget, no friends on the field." Later he made a typical Gunney breakthrough leaving myself, all 8½ stones, between him and the try-line. The only way I could see of stopping his burly frame was to give him a crack upstairs. I took off like a Spitfire. Geoff, with the ball tucked under his left arm caught me with his right hand, threw me into touch, scored his try and came back to where I was laying. He picked me up like a baby doll saying, "You're right, Stevie, no friends on the field".'

Gunney went with Great Britain on one Rugby League tour to Australia and later, in 1957, for a World Cup series. He decided that his most memorable Test match was on the first occasion he played against Australia, and considering his youthfulness — he was only 21 at the time — it was not a surprising choice. He remarked that the team spirit which develops in a Test team is indescribable;

the atmosphere tense, muscles straining and body keyed-up to a tension breaking limit. To have been privileged to have lived these moments is to have experienced, to him, ecstasy.

When I asked him for his most memorable match at club level he replied that there were at least fifty—did I want them all?! After much memory searching he chose a match that Hunslet lost—the Cup Final at Wembley against Wigan in 1965, with a score of 20-16. The issue was in doubt until the whistle and it was the close-run issue which makes it an outstanding personal memory.

'And your hardest match?' Facetiously he suggested when he was persuaded on Scarborough beach to participate in a game of push-ball. Seriously, he thought it must be the game against Whitehaven in a cup-tie the exact year of which he could not remember. After that match, in the bath, and for the only time in his long career, he momentarily decided he never wanted to play rugger again. 'There was an icy blast blowing straight down the pitch which was already under two inches of water, mixed with patches of ice. To say fingers were numb would be the understatement of sporting memories. Two players passed out at half-time. Shortly afterwards I appealed to the referee and didn't mince my words "For God's sake, ref, call it off." "Play on," was his answer and we did, the full 80 minutes. I couldn't feel the hot water in that bath after the game. In spite of my vow I was as eager as ever for the kick off when next Saturday came round.'

He is proud that in the summer of 1964 he was awarded the Windsor Trophy for the best and fairest player in the Rugby League for the previous season. That was an honour worth winning. Next season was the only occasion in his distinguished career he was sent off—by his own act of dismissal! 'It was against Wakefield. mentioning no names, two players had tackled me much too violently for my liking. It was the only time someone had really upset me and I considered it had been done deliberately with malice aforethought. I appealed to the referee for justice and he merely replied—"Play the ball". I did this and then strode across to the main offender, hit him and walked off without being asked! I suppose I can still fairly claim that I was never *sent* off. At least that was the only blot on my copybook!'

'And injuries?'

'I've had a broken rib, cracked a collar bone, two cartlidges removed, twenty broken noses and I've a compressed disc in my back but I've really been lucky. Oh—broken fingers and knocked-up thumbs don't count. And you shouldn't count broken noses really. I remember when I first broke my nose I went to the touch line for attention and they called the club doctor from his seat on the stand. I told him I thought I had broken my nose. "Why are you telling me," he asked "Go back and break his!"

'Do you think sportsmanship in the Rugby League has

deteriorated in recent years with the higher financial rewards at stake?'

'Sportsmanship to my mind is still the same; still, in the main, with an esprit-de-coeur between players, but individual skills are not visible because personal idiosyncrasies have been "coached" out. There is more coaching than ever now, far too much in my opinion. To young players I would say that if you have the aptitude for the game take every possible opportunity to develop it. Practice...... practice......practice. A rugby footballer must live the game but that doesn't mean he should not develop some hobbies outside. He should for *all* work makes Jack a dull boy and that applies equally as well to a professional footballer.'

Gunney practices what he preaches. Modern music, jazz, jive was, and is, to him a relaxation. They called him the 'Rock and Roll' forward when Hunslet played away. His gramophone always accompanied him in the club coach. He is also fond of fishing. 'I like my Sunday fishing—I feel better mentally and physically. I used to enjoy too going shooting with Jackie Charlton in his Leeds United days.'

It was obvious that all who knew 'Mr Hunslet' felt that his many awards would not have been complete without recognition at a national level. That came on 10th November 1970 when he went to Buckingham Palace for a well-merited M.B.E. That crowned a career outstanding in its skill, its sportsmanship, its loyalty and its ever-present eager willingness to help others. His last appearance for Hunslet in 1974 was his 600th senior game with them. An incredible record and even then he had to hand on the torch to ...... his wife. She was appointed secretary for the New Hunslet club on 3rd June 1974. Alas, Parkside was built over, the myrtle, white and flame men had a shared home at the Elland Road Greyhound track and now they are looking for a fresh field which all who love the game hope will, one day, re-echo the 'swept the seas' chorus once more. Wherever the Hunslet colours appear 'Mr (and Mrs!) Hunslet' will be remembered.

The Rugby League games between Hunslet and Leeds had to be experienced to be believed. The clashes between the two clubs were reminiscent of the Wars of the Roses cricketing contests between Yorkshire and Lancashire, 'Nowt to do with foreigners from other parts' being the attitude of the majority of the spectators. We have been to Gunney's headquarters and we must now move on to visit Headingley, the ground shared by Yorkshire County Cricket club and Leeds Rugby League club. Who is landlord and who is tenant I have not troubled to unravel for after all this is not meant to be a legal tome. Headingley—where a famous name amongst Rugby League celebrities once sat in the Leeds managerial chair—Edward Marsden Waring M.B.E. When I spoke to Willis Hall he mentioned that he was an **Eddie Waring** fan and that he had referred to him in *My Sporting Life*. Willis was one of thousands of the Eddie Waring Appreciation Society. Eddie had certainly come a long way since his Headingley days, but still had a Leeds home which he used for his regular broadcasting from the Leeds B.B.C. studios in Woodhouse Lane.

When one heard his cheery voice and saw his big smile as he began his rugby commentary it was difficult to realise that he was not a young man. Before coming to Leeds, Eddie Waring lived in Dewsbury. He attended Eastborough School in the town and his teenage days were centred between the Methodist Chapel and Rugby League football. It was the latter that took him into local journalism specialising in sports writing. He became coach eventually to the Dewsbury club and went on to become its manager. From there he arrived at Headingley in June 1944, as the new Leeds manager, but he was only destined to rule for a little over twelve months. The war was over and the *Yorkshire Evening News* tempted him on to their sports-writing staff, with additional facilities for free-lance work with the B.B.C. He was assigned by his paper to cover the first Rugby League tour to Australia after the war. Getting to Australia was not easy but he managed to secure a passage out on an aircraft carrier—H.M.S. *Indomitable*. The Royal Navy in some mysterious Service manner calculated the fare down to the coppers—it was exactly £11 11s 2d. What is more surprising is that they carried passengers at all! Eddie was by no means the only one for he has told how during the voyage he witnessed the roughest game—R.L. Tests and Wembley Cup Finals not excluded—of his life. A game of seven-a-side deck hockey between Wigan Wallopers and ......seven priests. The moment of chance, seen so frequently for the personalities we have so far met, occurred on his second tour with Great Britain's R.L. side to the Antipodes in 1951. He met Bob Hope, the American comedian, on the return journey and a friendship developed. Hope told him that television was the coming thing and if he wished to really succeed he should try to get into it.

Back in England he went down to the Rugby Union's holy of holies, Twickenham, and watched the commentators at work, made his plans for his own brand of commentating and obtained a foothold. He realised that to the rest of the country, the Rugby League was a mysterious northern rite and that an unorthodox approach would be the key to unlock the mystery. What has Jimmy Savile told us?—'If you want to be noticed, be different.' Eddie was different in more than one way. His northern accent, like Wilfred Pickles' before him, had that homely honest timbre that *made* you look and listen—his infectious and now so well-known chuckle, but above all the enthusiastic relish, the inward delight he managed to convey, as he described those crunching clashes of the giants below his box high up in the stand. How he laid the scene for a penalty kick in the air, under cover of which the pack of forwards rush menacingly on the unfortunate individual waiting interminably for the ball to drop into his hands and his body to be submerged under several giants. 'Up and under' he gleefully roared; and millions of viewers laughed with excitement at the spectacle. 'Up and under' has become a maxim fused with current language of our times.

From his expert knowledge of the League game he knows that those twenty-six players have a zest for what they are doing; that he and they know that enthusiasm is what life is all about. It is that reality which he has set out to get over on the air.....and succeeded. But spontaneous as it sounds, it did not happen just like that. Before every commentary he researched, 'did his homework' he terms it, and turned up at the ground at least one and a half hours before kick-off to assure himself that as far as possible nothing would go wrong. Eddie Waring has enthusiasm and that is the secret of his popularity. Enthusiasm. I met him for the first time shortly after the war when he was a journalist. It was at the Dewsbury ground and I still recall coming away with an impression of the then young Eddie Waring. Enthusiasm. He oozed it.

He drives himself ceaselessly. He has done 35 commentaries in a season and in January 1980 notched up his 500th. He did not miss a Wembley R.L. cup final since he commenced his commentaries in 1951. His favourite final was the match chosen by Geoff. Gunney as his most memorable—the 1965 Hunslet-Wigan affair. 'A cracking final' was his verdict. It must have been some match.

But he has faced criticism as well as enjoyed praise. In 1971 a team of fact-finding consultants considered the televising of Rugby League games and the commentaries provided. Their opinion was that the B.B.C. had been unfortunate in its choice of commentators because of the northern accent. From the north—and the demarcation line must have been drawn through Watford and the West country—came howls of protest. The wrath of the Eddie Waring Appreciation Societies was roused. The consultants crept back into their shells wondering just how daft they could have become so wrong. They were not heard again.

In his younger days he sang with the chapel choir. He loved 'to bellow out' (the verb is his own) the 'Messiah', so beloved of northerners. One of his memories of a Sydney R.L. Test match was travelling to the ground in the team coach and the fervour with which those tough young men sang 'Guide me, O Thou Great Jehovah'. As one pictures that scene in imagination how one wishes it could have been shared.

There is a generosity and humility too about Eddie which is good to see. He has been instrumental in raising more than £140,000 for players' benefit funds; he has given freely of his time for charity appeals; and has responded in many other ways to show of his care and concern for those less fortunate than himself. He is reluctant to talk about them, would like them to be forgotten but one incident will illustrate his simple humanity. Not so long ago a nineteen year old Cornish boy met with a road accident and sustained serious head injuries. He was in a coma. The hospital doctors were told that in addition to being a keen Rugby Union player the youngster was also an Eddie Waring fan. 'If Eddie would make a special recording which we could play back to the boy it might just strike a chord. It might help bring him out of his unconsciousness.' Eddie readily did what he was asked and his satisfaction was unbounded when he learnt the experiment had been a success. The boy recognised the familiar voice and eventually made a good recovery. Bob Hope certainly did Britain a good turn when he suggested television as the road to fame for Eddie Waring.

Headingley—the cricketing side of the ground now—has happy memories for thousands of Leeds schoolboys who were not slow to avail themselves of a privilege accorded to Yorkshire County Cricket Club members. With their membership ticket they could be accompanied to a match by a lady or child free of further charge and it was a rejuvenating sight to see swarms of schoolboys and girls patiently waiting outside the members' entrance to find a 'foster-father' big-hearted enough to see them inside.....and then lose them. They were not usually disappointed and once inside the ground they had close contact with the pavilion, autograph book at the ready with their 'gods' Sutcliffe, Hutton, Leyland, Verity, Bowes, Close—the list is endless. And when they wearied a little of the match they could always wander round the ground and make a copper or two picking up empty lemonade and beer bottles and return them to the refreshment kiosks. Many a youngster has had to dodge a cuff as he took a bottle that had not finally quenched its owner's thirst and many another has arrived home with more money in his pocket than when he left home in the morning!

In that mood of nostalgia we meet two of the great cricketing names who came from homes within the surrounds of Leeds. As a tribute to all cricketers who served in the World War I and II, and in particular to those who made the supreme sacrifice, we think of the late **Hedley Verity**—Captain Verity of the Green Howards. Donald Bradman said of Hedley Verity, 'He was not only a very great England and Yorkshire cricketer, he was also a gallant soldier, and chivalrous gentleman.' What a tribute from the finest batsman the world has known. But if Verity could have heard those words I am sure he would have liked the ending best of all—'a chivalrous gentleman', for that is what he was.

Whilst it is usual to associate Leeds with Rawdon, he could claim to be a 'loiner' from the inner city for he was born on 18th May 1905 in Brudenell Road, not a long way from the Headingley ground. His father was a coal merchant at Rawdon, chairman of the district council and a lay preacher at Benton Congregational church. Hedley was eight years of age when he was first taken to see Yorkshire play at Headingley and he quickly adopted George Hirst, Wilfred Rhodes and Jack Hobbs as his boyhood heroes. And what adulatory worship a boy gave to these god-like figures before money and sponsorship, one-day games, knock-out competitions, 'cissified helmets' (as another great cricketer from Nottingham, Bill Voce described current cricketing headgear recently) and many other regretted activities turned a great game into a travesty of its true self. A set of dog-eared cigarette cards collected from a Gold Flake or Players packet was a boy's pre-war dream of affluence.

When Hedley was sixteen he practised with the students of Rawdon Baptist Theological College. At seventeen he was good enough to play for Rawdon (Yorkshire Council) XI, determined to play for Yorkshire as a batsman. He practised endlessly and assiduously in front of a mirror, trying to perfect his strokes. The same year that he played for Rawdon he received official acknowledgement of his potentiality—or so it would seem to a teenager—he was called to the Yorkshire 'nets'. The following year he was Rawdon's first wicket batsman, and the Yorkshire Council is a league in which it is worth while playing. In 1926 he was playing with Yorkshire Colts, and George Hirst, who had the young players under his wing and had converted him to bowling, recommended him to a Lancashire League club—Accrington. After one season with them, he joined Middleton for three seasons and then Wilfred Rhodes retired. Hedley got his big chance—his first opportunity to play for Yorkshire. His boyhood dream come true but his ambitions realised as a bowler rather than as a batsman. That first match was on 21st May 1930 at Huddersfield and Sussex were being played in friendly fashion. His first championship game followed at Hull against Leicestershire, with a successful 8 wickets taken for 60 runs. His friendship with Bill Bowes began, for he too had joined Yorkshire's first eleven just a little earlier.

1931 was his first full season with the county and he had only played in fourteen games when he took the bowler's 'gold'—all ten wickets in an innings for 36 runs. The 16th May 1931 was an historic date because at Headingley, the venue of this match against Warwickshire, the feat had never before been achieved. Indeed, it had happened only twice before in Yorkshire's history. After only thirty games he was in the England team to play New Zealand. The New Zealanders said at the end of the tour that Verity, Bowes and F.R. Brown were the best bowlers against whom they had played, whilst 'Wisden' selected Hedley as one of the five cricketers of the year—in his first full season at county level.

In 1932 he again performed the unsurpassable at Headingley—how he must have loved that ground—against Nottinghamshire. All ten wickets for just ten runs and at one period in this feat, he sent down fifteen deliveries, took seven wickets—including the 'hat-trick'—and had but three runs scored off him. It was rightly described — and the description must surely still apply — as the finest piece of bowling ever accomplished in the cricketing world. The newspaper headline was 'Verity of Veritys, all is Verity'. It earned for him, from his biographer, Sam Davis, the title of 'Prince with a piece of leather'.

When Holmes and Sutcliffe scored that mammoth 555 for 1 against Essex at Leyton, before Sutcliffe decided to call it a day and virtually gave his wicket away, was it *quite* fair of Verity to rub salt into a stinging wound with 5 for 8 and 5 for 45?! Of course it was. Yorkshire play cricket to win. The following year one can almost imagine Essex trembling in their white boots as the Yorkshire fixture came round. Hedley didn't disappoint. He took seventeen of their wickets for 91 — all in one day and again at Leyton. Horses for courses? Cricketers for Counties.

Some cricketing experts, before he went on his first Australian tour, felt he would not find their wickets to his liking, but whether in England or Australia he dealt with the Aussie batsman equally efficiently. At Perth, on his first tour, against a combined Australian XI, he had 6 for 28 before lunch, including 'the Don', whose wicket he took in all ten times. At Lords in 1934 he equalled Rhodes' then record of 15 wickets in an Australian Test, 15 for 104 and having taken fourteen of them in one day.

He had practised before a mirror as a future batsman and he had his reward with one century for Yorkshire against Jamaica in 1936. He was equally meticulous in his bowling practice. In season and out of season he would send down ball after ball aiming for a precise spot. His philosophy as a bowler was a philosophy for life for everyone. He believed that no matter the achievements of the past, the assurance of the present, or the promise for the future, there must never be an end to endeavour or to learning. He was a little more proficient than he was yesterday — a little less so than he would be tomorrow. His advice to young bowlers was Kiplinesque, 'Don't get despondent when the luck of the game is against you, when everything seems to be going wrong. Keep a stout heart and keep on trying.'

The 1939 war was looming on the near horizon, when he went on to the field at Hove and took seven Sussex wickets for 9 runs — his swan song and the second best analysis of his brief but enthralling career. As he returned to the pavilion with the war clouds thickening he said, 'I wonder if I shall ever bowl here again.'

It was a prophetic utterance. His final figures could have been written that day — for Yorkshire, 3,883 wickets and for England, in 40 Tests, 144 wickets; and five times head of the bowling averages. A truly great cricketer who proved himself to be an equally fine soldier. On the outbreak of war he was commissioned with the Green Howard Regiment and later with the rank of Captain went to the Middle East. He took part in the fighting of the North African campaign and in the Sicilian landings. In a night attack on the 19th July 1943 he was wounded. Apparently, enemy fire had set light to a cornfield and his silhouetted body presented a target which was not missed. His batman stayed with him throughout the night, rendering what aid and comfort he could. They were both found at dawn by a German officer and Hedley was taken to Casserto Hospital in Italy. He received the best possible surgical treatment at the hands of Italian surgeons and appeared to be responding to treatment. On the eighth day after extensive surgery he had a relapse and died on the 31st July. After he had been buried another Yorkshire cricketer Frank Smailes helped raise a cross over the grave—a cross on which was carved the white rose of Yorkshire. At the time, Bill Bowes was a prisoner of war at a camp in Chieti, also in Italy. Two colonials in the camp had picked up news that a cricketer had died of wounds—'A guy called Verity I think', said one of them in Bowes' hearing. 'Say that again. *Was* the name Verity? Was it a cricketer?' 'Sure, yes, that's right.' Bill Bowes bowed his head. A noble christian gentleman had passed on. His team mate.

Partisanship is not lacking in Pudsey and in a township which considers itself a separate entity tucked away between Leeds and Bradford, it may not favour one of its own being even considered for a book dealing with personalties from Leeds and its surrounds. At the risk of displeasure I feel **Sir Leonard Hutton** must be included. Not in depth for many pens have recorded his triumphs but sufficient to let the many who followed his fortunes in his halcyon days know that their old favourite is not forgotten.

He was the youngest of four sons of Henry and Lily Hutton and was born at Fulneck, Pudsey, on 23rd June 1916—almost with a cricket bat in his hand. He first played club cricket, alongside his father, with Fulneck Sunday School. From there he went into the Pudsey St. Lawrence 2nd XI at the age of *twelve* and not long after was promoted to their first team. He was only thirteen when his call came to the Headingley 'nets' and George Hirst quickly and whole-heartedly recommended him to the County Committee. Hirst was not usually lavish in praise—Yorkshiremen seldom are—but he recognised that here was a rare diamond in his annual collection of youngsters. 'Hutton—you cannot fault his method.' That was the opening gambit in a never ceasing pattern of praise that followed him throughout his career.

Len reflected the Yorkshire tradition of endless practice, studying style and perfecting technique until in 1934 he was ready to step out of the Yorkshire dressing room for his first walk to the wicket as a first-teamer. If it seemed a long walk out it must have seemed a longer walk back for he had scored a 'duck'. That did not make headline news but some years later I remember coming out of an office adjacent to City Square and the newspaper seller at the side of the Queen's Hotel had a small crowd round him eagerly buying the *Evening Post*—pre-transistor days, of course. What calamity had befallen us now? I then saw his glaring placard—'HUTTON—A DUCK'. But in 1934 Hutton wiped his first O from memory with a youthful masterpiece—196 against Worcestershire, the first of his 129 centuries for county and country.

Against Australia at the Oval on 20th August 1938 began the most famous century for England of all times. Young Hutton—he was only just turned 22—batted all through the first day and the second. On the morning of the third England and the world were in agony. Only one question was on everyone's lips, 'Would Hutton pass Bradman's Test record of an innings of 334 runs?' It is impossible to imagine his feelings as he walked out of the Oval pavilion that morning at 11.30. Every ball was described over the air; every bus driver, every lorry driver, everyone who could not be near a wireless set at every possible opportunity asked anyone within earshot, 'Is he still in?' 'How many?' The suspense was ended at 12.45 p.m.—pandemonium broke loose on the Surrey ground. Len—Yorkshire's Len—HAD DONE IT! After 13 hours 20 minutes the discipline demanded by the longest display of concentration ever seen in a Test match was over—he was finally out for 364, a world record that was to stand for many years until Gary Sobers passed it by just one run.

Between 1934 and the outbreak of war he scored 25 centuries for his county and one wonders what his total would have been but for the six years' cricketing vacuum that followed. For a man who depended on his arms for carrying on his craft it was an unfortunate accident on an Army commando course which led to his left arm being broken and being set and re-set. He was put under the care of the Leeds surgeon Mr R. Broomhead who found it necessary to put it into plaster no less than twelve times and even he could only give him an arm permanently fore-shortened. Thankfully it did not affect his superlative skill and when peace returned he was there to take his rightful place for Yorkshire and England.

1949 was one of his vintage years and he had scored his 1,000 runs for the season as early as the 9th of June. That was the month he went on to break the record for the number of runs scored in a calendar month. The venue was Headingley and on that last day of the month I can remember the thrill of watching him walk to the wicket knowing he needed 80 runs and if he had failed by only one run this particular record might never again be within his grasp. What an eternity it seemed. One was almost driven *not* to watch each ball as it was bowled, but I think it is safe to say that Hutton was the calmest man at Headingley that day. I was certainly well down the list. At last the record breaking stroke was made and bedlam broke loose as it had done at the Oval. Len had done it again. He finished the month with 1,254 runs, in the August 1,050 runs and finished with 3,429, the highest total made in one season in first class cricket by any Yorkshire player, although Herbert Sutcliffe had, in 1932, set him 3,362 to beat.

When Hutton announced his retirement during the winter of 1955-56—although he actually played his last first class game in 1960—he had been the first professional to captain England and served in this capacity against Australia, New Zealand, India, Pakistan and West Indies. One record which no doubt he would have been pleased not to have earned was that of being the only cricketer given out 'Obstructing the field' in a Test match—the famous occasion in 1951 when he collided with the wicket-keeper who was attempting a catch. His was a comparatively early retirement from cricket, but he the master craftsman had scored 40,140 runs. On 1st January 1956 he received in addition to his many cricketing honours the national accolade of a knighthood. The twelve year old Pudsey St Lawrence 2nd XI schoolboy cricketer had carried out his bat as Sir Leonard Hutton.

The cricketing world, and the world in its widest sense, felt it a well-deserved honour. They wish him many more years to reflect on his achievements. He has brought our local sporting reminiscences to a close—rewritten twenty years hence, I am certain Leeds will have had sportsmen of equal merit from which to choose.

BIBLIOGRAPHY

The Crown Point Story—the story of Alf Cooke Ltd, A.J. Turner (1966).

St. Michael—a History of Marks and Spencers, Goronwy Rees (1969).

Schofield Golden Jubilee (Schofields Ltd., 1951).

Ideal in Industry, being the Story of Montague Burton, ed. Ronald Redmayne (1936).

I Travel the Road, Robert Barr (1945).

Geoffrey, J.E. Appleyard (1945).

Everest—The Hard Way, Chris Bonnington (1976).

Henry Moore, John Russell (1968).

Journey from the North, Storm Jameson (1969).

The Autobiography of a Journalist, William Linton Andrews (1964).

Speaking to Each Other (2 vols.), Richard Hoggart (1970).

The Uses of Literacy, Richard Hoggart (1970).

As it Happened, Jimmy Savile (1976).

Edge of Darkness, Edge of Light, R.C. Scriven (1977).